WHAT ELSE IS POSSIBLE?

WHAT ELSE IS POSSIBLE?

A MAGICIAN'S SECRETS
to Greater Breakthroughs
in Your Life and Work

DEVIN HENDERSON

WHAT ELSE IS POSSIBLE?
A Magician's Secrets to Greater Breakthroughs in Your Life and Work

Book Cover Design by Abigael Elliott
Interior Layout and Design by Stephanie Anderson
Editorial Team: Traci Matt, Donnel McLohon

ISBNs:
979-8-89165-253-8 *Paperback*
979-8-89165-254-5 *Hardback*
979-8-89165-252-1 *E-book*

Published by:
Streamline Books
Kansas City, MO
shareyourstory.com

For Lynn, Claire, Charlotte, Cambry,
Elsie, Eva, Emme, Haven & Ivy

CONTENTS

Foreword by Mark Mayfield ix

INTRODUCTION: Seeing Potential over Limitation 1

1   Start Ugly, Start Small, Pick Up the Ball 9

2   A Seemingly Impossible Goal 21

3   The Possibility Mindset 29

4   My Magical Journey 45

5   An Invitation from *America's Got Talent* 63

6   A Whole New Meaning to AGT 73

7   Pause, Pivot, Pull 83

8   What's Your Magic? 97

9   Share Your Magic 109

10   The Blessing of Imperfection 123

EPILOGUE: Some Possibilities Live Into Eternity 139

Acknowledgments 145

About the Author 149

FOREWORD

WHEN I WAS asked by Devin to write a foreword to his book, I was honored. So here was my first draft:

Devin is cool.

He said it needed to be longer. So here was my second draft:

Devin is really cool.

Then he explained what it should entail. I didn't know. I'd never written one. So . . .

This is my official foreword. Every book has one. Personally, I think it's spelled wrong. It must be spelled with an "e" in the middle to make it special. It is special. And important. On occasion, it can be the only thing read in a book, because if it's awful, it can cause people to go no further. It's like the trailer for a movie. It better grab your interest, or you won't be at the theater later eating some twenty-dollar popcorn.

So, there's a lot of pressure on this foreword, but I accept it, because this book and this author are worth it. Trust me on this.

I'll bet my Ovaltine decoder ring on it. I'm that confident you need, and will enjoy, this book.

Full disclosure . . . I'm old. Not gonna say how old, but I was born shortly after they invented dirt. And I'm jaded. That often happens when you've been around the block to infinity and beyond. I'm telling you these things because I'm not easily impressed with much of anything, or anybody, these days. But I am with Devin and his message that something greater is always possible. It's impressive. It can change you.

It's seldom you find a speaker that can immediately grab your attention and never lose it. It's equally rare to know an author who delivers impact with every word. It's nearly impossible to find an individual who can do both.

But enough about me—I'm here to write about Devin. (Sorry, attempting to keep your attention with some levity . . . the pressure of writing this foreword is immense, and I'm trying anything.)

Seriously, that's Devin Henderson. A great speaker *and* a great author. He's one of the most talented, smart, funny, decent, inspirational human beings I've ever met. Truth be known, there is some subliminal jealousy in this writing. (I hope he doesn't read this.) Now, his spoken word is complemented with a written one and he's sharing his wisdom in this book. Take advantage of reading insights from this brilliant magician, mentalist, comedian, writer, and speaker. You are lucky to have picked up this book. Don't waste the opportunity.

Devin is a teacher. And I've always thought the best teachers illuminate their lessons with real-life experiences. That's what makes a message relatable. That's what makes a message "stick." Devin's accomplishments *and* disappointments do just that. He and his message are memorable. They inspire action.

I could spend hours writing of Devin's virtues, as I've admired his performances for years. I'm a borderline stalker. I do that with people who impress me. However, when I first saw the title, *What Else Is Possible?* I was suspect. As I said earlier, I'm jaded. But because of my long-standing admiration, I decided to give it a chance. Good call on my part. It's brilliant.

I wish I had read this book when I was younger. It would have saved me countless peccadillos. (That's a fun word to Google.) Since I'm much older, that would have required Devin to write it as an infant, so it might not have been quite as good. But if I could time travel, I'd take this book back to my younger self and tell him to pore over every chapter. To learn how to handle setbacks. To keep a healthy perspective on everything that happens. To always be thankful. I would have been a better and smarter and happier me.

One more thing: This book is not the traditional, cliché-driven, platitude-filled, motivational diatribe. It's a hands-on, practical guide for how to make greater things happen for you. Even after a major disappointment. It will help you realize that *today is the first day of the rest of your life.* Wait, that's a cliché. But Devin didn't say it, I did. I'm just trying to make the point that we all have times when it's difficult to recover, refocus, and rebound. Devin gives you the tools to do just that, because something greater is always possible.

—**MARK MAYFIELD,** Hall of Fame Speaker

Seeing Potential over Limitation

THE FACT THAT you picked up this book tells me something about you: You're drawn to greatness. To innovation. To opportunity. Whether you've just experienced the best year of your life or the hardest one, you're not standing still. You're ready to move forward, to unlock new levels of potential you haven't even tapped into yet.

And what if I told you there's a surefire way to make that happen? A single, powerful sentence. One question strong enough to reshape the course of your life—and the lives of those around you.

Are you ready to discover it? Here it is:

What else is possible?

Have you ever asked yourself that question? When you were young, future possibilities may have seemed endless. But as you reached your teen years and started mapping out career and personal goals, perhaps—like me—you felt overwhelmed by the vast number of choices. And as life moved forward, have you found that daily stressors and major events slowly narrowed your once-bright vision of unlimited success? In the following pages, I'm confident you'll be inspired to embrace your biggest ambitions once again—to realign, to recharge.

What else is possible?

Consider this question a multifunction tool, like a Swiss Army knife that can tighten a screw, hammer in a nail, or trim nose hairs (I'm only kidding, there's no hammer on those things). Well, just like a Swiss Army knife has many uses, asking what else is possible can enable you to move smoothly through day-to-day personal and professional opportunities with more resourcefulness and decisiveness. It can inspire you to achieve extraordinary things. It can help you celebrate when your hard work has finally paid off. And in your darkest moments—when you're stuck in the metaphorical wilderness of life's chaos, demands, and disappointments—this one question might just save your life.

So what else is possible? Thankfully, the answer is as exciting and easy to understand as the question.

Something greater is always possible.

If you believed that every single day, can you imagine what things would look like for you in all aspects of your world? What if your life could be bigger, richer, and more satisfying than you have ever envisioned? It absolutely can be. Greater collaboration, greater potential, and having a greater impact are well within your reach, because even when you can't see it, and no matter what is going on around you, something greater is always possible.

Now, before I go on, I want to point out that I am not suggesting you should be in a constant grind to achieve a vision, regardless of what effect it has on those you love, your own well-being, or other aspects of your life. On the contrary, to keep your attention and intentions in check, I strongly believe it is vital to practice regular moments of R&R, counting your blessings, and knowing when to take longer pauses in your journey toward excellence. Sure, oftentimes pursuing greater possibilities focuses on external achievements and metrics, but sometimes it's simply about creating awareness and acceptance regarding your current position.

Picture the *something greater is always possible* ideal opening up a world of positivity for you to explore. Making room for peace and contentment. Shedding light on the path for your next step. Can you imagine feeling focused and confident even while experiencing your hardest situations? Greater possibilities will unfold for you internally and externally as you expose illusions such as doubt and uncertainty with the truth that something greater is indeed in your future.

Why do I believe something greater is always possible for you? My own experience has taught me that in every area of life, mindset determines if and when you rise above challenging circumstances and roadblocks. If you can respond to anxiety, uncertainty, or just plain exhaustion with *What else is possible?* you will never stop moving forward. Peace, clarity, and endless energy are all within reach if you believe in the hope of possibility.

Ever since I was a kid kicking a soccer ball around in my hometown of Shawnee, Kansas, I have applied this principle over and over and experienced some exciting things as a result. From excelling in my soccer hobby, to winning awards as a magician and comedian, to becoming a professional keynote speaker, believing something greater is always possible has always powered my drive. My life has been the result of consistently embracing the what-ifs,

3

including being a blessed dad to eight daughters. Eight is *not* a typo, nor is daughters. And yes, I *love* being a girl dad.

Now, maybe the word *magician* caught you off guard. Or maybe when you saw it in the subtitle, you thought this was a book for people wanting to learn how to do card tricks or pull rabbits from hats. But no—this isn't a how-to-magic guide. It's for anyone pursuing something greater in life. So how does magic fit into all of this? Let me explain—because once you understand that piece, the rest of the book will make a whole lot more sense.

The short story is that back in 2004, before I ever stepped onstage as a speaker, I began performing professionally as a magician. (Some people prefer the term "illusionist," since I obviously don't attempt to practice actual "wizardry." But in this book, I'll use the terms "magic trick" and "illusion" interchangeably.) About seven years into my career as a magician, someone encouraged me with the idea that I have more than just entertainment to share with the world. They told me to explore what positive factors have contributed to my success as a performer and how I might share those ideas to help others experience similar victories. That conversation changed everything.

I started leaning into my deeper message, using magic not just to entertain but to illustrate real-life truths. Today, I'm truly living my purpose as a motivational keynote speaker who uses illusions as metaphors to help people visualize and believe in the seemingly impossible in all they do. The magic adds a layer of fun and interaction . . . but more importantly, the magic makes my message more memorable (alliteration not intended).

A Magician's Secrets Revealed?

Have you ever heard the expression, "Magicians never reveal their secrets?" Well, I'm sharing mine. Not the secrets behind the illusions—as a rule of thumb, those stay protected. The secrets

I'm revealing are far more valuable: practical insights that lead to greater breakthroughs in your life and work. These insights didn't appear out of thin air. They are lessons I've learned through decades of performing magic—and through real-life moments that have stretched, challenged, and refined me along the way.

And by the way: You might be surprised by what *does* get revealed.

That said, you will discover how to become the best version of yourself. And to better engage with you, I'll be describing some of the illusions I perform—giving you a kind of virtual front row seat to my in-person keynote experience. "Unreal," "unexpected," and "unforgettable" are words people often use to describe these moments. But the illusions go deeper than just entertainment—they're tools to help you visualize, internalize, and ultimately transform how you approach every part of your life.

In fact, I'll give you an example right now and put my money where my mouth is. I mean that literally, because it's a trick using money.

A Great Investment

The reason I'm including this trick in the introduction is because it's how I currently begin my keynote; not to mention it's a *great* way to illustrate the power of seeing potential over limitation. Here's how the trick goes:

I present a stack of five $1 bills to the audience, which they can see perfectly because I use a close-up camera on stage that projects the image onto the big screens. High tech, I know. As I count the $1 bills, rather than counting 1, 2, 3, I count by twenties: *20, 40, 60* . . . which gets a laugh from the audience.

I then explain that I am not delusional—just optimistic. I say, "It's fun. Try counting these $1s as twenties." Now imagine as I count the five $1s again that the entire audience is counting out loud with me: "20, 40, 60 . . ." Everyone laughs and has a great time with this. One crowd even got crazy and counted, "1,000,000, 2,000,000, 3,000,000 . . ." and I said, "Yeah baby, let's go big!"

I then say, "And just like these bills, each of you has the potential to increase your own value, the value of your team, and the value of your entire organization. By investing in yourself—through gaining confidence, learning and developing your skills—you can amplify your worth and unlock greater possibilities." At this point, I snap my fingers, and the $1 bills instantly turn into $20 bills! It's shocking and amazing. I clearly show that every single bill is now a $20 bill and that I'm hiding nothing.

I then explain, "But this transformation didn't happen by itself, and neither will yours. It takes focus and the belief that you're worth the investment. When you commit to that, your personal value will multiply like magic! But if you're not careful, it can diminish just as easily." As I say this, I give the $20 bills a little shake and they suddenly turn back into $1s.

"Self-doubt, negative habits, and neglecting self-growth can take away from your worth and effectiveness. You have the potential to be powerful, impactful, and valuable. But if you let those negative factors take over, you're giving up parts of yourself that matter most. But the good news is that you can always reclaim your value and level up in powerful ways when you ask the question, *What else is possible?*"

Then, with a simple riffle of the $1 bills, I transform them into $100s. This transformation is so visual it never fails to get a round of applause. By the way, can you see now why I love my job?

I conclude the metaphor with: "So, if you know your value can grow—or shrink—how do you stay in control of that? And how do you make sure you're always moving toward something greater?"

This book is intended to help you answer those questions. And to run with the money analogy, in what ways *can* you "invest" in yourself and others in a way that will ignite untapped potential? What is the key to unlocking your greatness? Well, first of all, spoiler alert—I don't hold all the answers to life. I know, disappointing and shocking. I am simply going to share with you the secrets that have allowed me to accomplish great things in my life and that I'm confident will help you do the same with yours. I truly desire for you to look past any possible lies and negativity you are making allowances for and, instead, see what could be. The principles you're about to learn will help you master hard things and rise through unexpected challenges at home and at work—to sustain forward progress. You will discover how to become the best you can be, both as an individual and as a member of the team (or teams) you belong to.

While this book shares many stories from my own journey, its true message is about *you*—and the people you impact every day. Whether you're an entrepreneur, a professional, a parent, or a volunteer, this is about *your* growth, *your* resilience, and *your* ability to thrive as you take on the next challenge.

It's about facing the impossible with confidence and skill. It's about turning setbacks—self-doubt, disappointment, even failure—into fuel for something greater. And most of all, it's about unlocking the boundless possibilities ahead of you—at work, in your community, with your friends and family, and within yourself.

So, are you ready to step up? To embrace the extraordinary? Now that you've got a magician in your corner, amazing things are about to happen. Let's make some magic.

What else is possible?

CHAPTER ONE

Start Ugly, Start Small, Pick Up the Ball

MY FIRST MEMORY of the power of possibilities came when I discovered soccer juggling at the age of seven.

No, wait a minute. My first memory of the power of possibilities was when I was five years old: I pointed my plastic magic sword toward the sky and called on the power of Grayskull. Apparently I *didn't* have the power, but I never gave up on the possibility of becoming He-Man. Maybe someday. Those days with the sword may have sparked my imagination, but it was soccer juggling that taught me three unforgettable truths. They became a mantra not just for sports, but for magic, business, parenting, and life.

Soccer juggling, or keepy uppy, as Bluey and Peppa Pig call it (three cartoon references already—it's clearly going to be a good book), is the solo sport of keeping the ball off the ground without using your hands and arms. The whole idea is to see how many kicks in a row you can get using your feet, knees, shoulders, and head before you drop the ball and have to start over.

When I was in first grade, my mom sent me to soccer camp. One morning, thinking I had signed up for a dribbling session— where you learn to move the ball down the field—I accidentally walked into a juggling lesson. The coach spread out this group of little boys on half the field and with the patience of a retired homeschool parent began to teach us how to keep the ball in the air. He taught us that the greatest soccer teams are made up of players who practice juggling behind the scenes, because learning control over the ball in this way transfers to more control of the ball in the actual game.

The coach's strategy was to start small. Kick the ball once, then catch it. Don't try to kick it twice. Kick it once, catch it. Learn how the ball responds to your kicks. *Easier than it sounds.* The first minutes of the session were eaten up by chasing down and picking up the ball. It was not pretty, to put it nicely. It was ugly, to put it meanly. But I immediately made adjustments. Once I learned to angle my foot properly, hit the ball with the correct part of my foot, and give it just the right touch, the ball went straight up, and I caught it! As I moved on to two kicks, the coach reiterated the start small idea: "Do not move onto three kicks until you master two," and so on. All of a sudden I was no longer concerned with dribbling, passing, or shooting. Juggling consumed my attention. By the end of that hour-long session I worked my way up to four kicks before dropping the ball—and I was hooked. So I went home and kept at it.

That obsession with improvement didn't stay on the soccer field—it followed me into every chapter of life, including the stage. In my keynotes, after I give a demonstration of soccer juggling, I often invite a volunteer to attempt the first steps of learning to juggle a soccer ball, just as I did. I've seen all kinds of people step forward, but my favorites are always the big guys in work boots who jump up, ready to give it a shot—it's happened more than once.

As I guide them through the "start small" process, the

transformation is powerful to watch. At first, they can barely kick the ball once and catch it. But with my coaching and the energy of the cheering audience, they start making small adjustments. Little by little, their confidence builds. Soon, they're kicking the ball multiple times in a row—sometimes close to ten!

It's an exciting moment, both for them and for the crowd. But the real takeaway is this: If they kept practicing, stayed focused, and committed to the process, there's no doubt they could surpass their own expectations. The only thing holding them back is time. And isn't that true for all of us? Our potential is limitless—if we're willing to persist.

Chasing 1,000

As for my young self, I worked very hard at it and stayed laser focused. A month after that first juggling lesson, I was up to 15 kicks. A year later I got 50. When I was ten, I got 250 kicks, which, if you would've asked me, was pretty great for a fourth grader. At that point perhaps most people would call it good and move onto exploring another activity, but I just kept asking, *What else is possible?* And so . . . I set a soccer juggling goal of 1,000 kicks.

I went to my dad because he was my champion, he was my cheerleader, and I wanted him to assure me it was doable. My dad was a Marine, and you know this: Once a Marine, always an uptight father (I couldn't resist—that joke always gets a laugh in my keynote). Being a Marine, coupled with growing up during the Great Depression (he was born in 1930 and was forty-nine years old when I was born—mind-blowing, I know), my dad knew something about determination and grit. I told him about my aspiration of 1,000 kicks and asked if he thought I could do it. This is what I heard: "You really want to know what I think? No, I don't think you can do it." Before we assign any shame to my dad, keep in mind, this man loved me and wanted the best for me, which is why he was being perfectly honest. He didn't want me to waste my time pursuing an activity that he didn't believe was possible and would only end in disappointment.

Has anyone ever told you, "That's not possible"? Maybe it was even a person who loves you and is rooting for you. Maybe it was a well-meaning parent who didn't want you to waste time on something he thought you'd never accomplish. Maybe it was an experienced coworker who loves to share warnings about things she has tried unsuccessfully. Maybe it was a spouse who has watched you fail before and doesn't have the capacity to deal with it again. Maybe it was even something you've told yourself. Many times, "That's not possible" is just not true, but if you listen to those negative voices, no matter how well intentioned, you might quit. Have you ever given up because you bought into someone else's discouraging opinion? Have you ever quit too early because your own self-doubt trumped the belief that you have what it takes to succeed?

Something greater is always possible for you no matter what anyone thinks, including yourself. I could have let my dad's words discourage me, but I refused to believe my goal was impossible, and I refused to quit. While he loved me enough to be blunt, I loved possibility enough to keep going.

When I was fifteen, I hit a significant milestone: 1,259 kicks! And you probably won't be surprised to hear that I didn't stop there. With the *what else is possible* mentality, I ultimately reached a juggling record I never imagined I would hit. Can you guess how many kicks? Most people at my live events guess 2,000 to 3,000. Child's play. A few years ago, I reached my all-time high of 11,241. Just to be clear, that's 11,241 consecutive kicks, without ever dropping the ball, over a two-hour period.

From there, I wondered what was possible beyond soccer juggling and simply counting kicks, and I discovered soccer freestyle. Soccer freestyle is when you add complicated tricks to the juggling.

It's a whole new level of athleticism and risk beyond mere keepy uppy. It's the next level of soccer juggling, to say the least. While juggling is a numbers game, freestyle is an art form. If you've ever seen tricks where soccer players catch the ball on the back of their neck or kick it with their legs crossed, or even juggle sitting down or lying on their back, that's soccer freestyle. I've even incorporated handstands and ball spinning. Think Harlem Globetrotters but mostly with your feet. I have spent hours upon hours and many years attempting to master each next maneuver.

Reflecting back on that day at soccer camp, I had no idea that the coach had planted the seeds of what would shape not only the course of my soccer journey but also my life. The perspective I gained from him has propelled me in everything from magic to speaking to parenting, and it can help you in everything you do, both personally and professionally:

1 **START UGLY.** Your first attempts will look clumsy; that's normal.
2 **START SMALL.** One kick, then catch. Master one before two.
3 **PICK UP THE BALL.** Every drop is an invitation to try again. Chase it down, scoop it up, and restart.

Decades later, those three principles converged into a single mantra that guides nearly everything I do:

Start ugly, start small, and pick up the ball.

Deep Dive: Start Ugly, Start Small

If you embrace the ideas of starting ugly and starting small, you've already removed the biggest barriers to progress: perfectionism, fear of embarrassment, and waiting for the "right time." Those barriers keep so many people from doing the very thing that could bring them joy and fulfillment. If your dream is to own your own business, take one step each day toward that goal. Maybe even start each morning by putting aside your lengthy to-do list and focusing on just one task: a task as simple as brainstorming names for the business or creating a mission statement. That's small, but it's better than promising yourself you'll write a whole plan some-day when it's the "perfect time." Small steps add up to big results.

Maybe your company just merged with another and your com-fortable work situation has suddenly become unpredictable. How do you deal with that? You start small. Get through the first day. Maybe introduce yourself to one new person and begin to develop a relationship. Or what about new software? You don't have to learn it all in one day. Perhaps you can learn one part at a time or reach out to someone who's familiar with it and schedule a help session.

If you decide to run a marathon, guess what, you don't have to wait until you have the perfect workout clothes or weather to start training. You could just get out there and run around the block, even if your form's not that good. Start ugly. Start small.

Maybe your goal is to retire before you reach fifty. You'll likely increase your chances for this if you start tracking expenditures and making investments early.

Perhaps your teenager wants to go far, far away to college. Sure, there are plenty of local schools, but her seemingly impossible goal is to study at Harvard or Stanford. Maybe now is the time to teach her that meeting that desire is possible! You could watch some videos from her toddler years, have a good cry, then wipe away the tears and start researching scholarships and housing options.

Do you deal with anxiety? If you simply struggle to get out of bed some days, start small. Can you throw the blankets off? Maybe make it to the shower? Then out the front door and into work? If you can, perhaps by the end of the day you will surprise yourself with what you've accomplished.

The key is to start, and sometimes that's not pretty. It can be downright ugly. But starting ugly doesn't mean being sloppy or careless. Sure, it might look sloppy to people on the outside who don't understand that you're simply being brave enough to take action rather than think about it forever, but your ultimate intention is to conquer this new endeavor. You can still *aim* for perfection, but starting ugly means being willing to start imperfectly. If you wait for perfection, you'll likely never launch that project or try something new. Only *you* can make the choice to start. When you start ugly, you can end beautifully. When you start small, you can end big.

Deep Dive: Pick Up the Ball

Achieving greatness is about not only your mindset but also what you practice every day. Once you start ugly and start small, the next thing you need to do is pick up the ball. Mistakes will be made. Dropping the ball is inevitable, which means you and your teammates must stay committed to picking it back up—and making the necessary *adjustments* along the way. That's the part we often overlook. If little me had not chased after the ball the first time it hit the ground *and* made some tweaks to my technique, you might not have this book in your hands. I don't even know how many times I've dropped the ball over the years to reach my current record, but my guess would be around infinity, give or take. And every time I picked it up again, I had to adjust—just a little. Angle the foot. Soften the touch. Learn from what didn't work.

As a leader, do you allow your people to start ugly? Are they encouraged to drop the ball, or are they, for a lack of better words, *punished* when they do so? When people are given freedom to explore, struggle, adjust, and try again, they are more likely to claim ownership in processes and projects, and their passion and creativity will flow unimaginably. On the flip side, when the

WHEN YOU START UGLY, YOU CAN END **BEAUTIFULLY.** WHEN YOU START SMALL, YOU CAN END BIG expectation is simply meeting the status quo, people may grow stale and move on to another job where they feel more valued.

Of course, there are jobs that require little to no room for error because of safety concerns and what's at stake. A facility manager shouldn't go around a power generation station yelling, "Drop the ball, everyone!" But the majority of the time, having the freedom for mistakes, making tweaks, and picking up the ball again is the difference between people and teams who consistently do extraordinary things and those who don't.

And it's not just *that* you pick up the ball—it's *how* you do it. Instead of grabbing it reluctantly and sluggishly, imagine picking it up with energy and excitement. Imagine responding to failure not just by refusing to quit, but by bouncing back with passion. That's where real growth happens. It's not about how many times you drop the ball—it's about how many times you pick it up, and how open you are to learning and adapting each time. Dropping the ball builds humility and reminds us that while we may aim for perfection, the real goal is progress. Consistently regrouping after failures—big and small—has helped me grow in every area of life, and it can do the same for you. Whether you're working toward the next level in relationships, professional goals, or even hobbies, keep picking up the ball with enthusiasm and keep fine-tuning as you go.

When it comes to achievement, some people say the hardest part is getting started. Maybe. Or maybe the hardest part is sticking with it and, in collaborative situations, sticking together. Imagine what it was like back at soccer camp. All the other kids shared in my excitement about that first kick, but after dropping the ball they were not quite as excited to run and pick it up, over and over again. Their desire to stay engaged with the coach and take their results to new heights began to wane after repeated failure. But my excitement only grew. Why? Because I was able to see beyond the initial failure to the inevitable breakthrough. I saw that every dropped ball gave me new feedback. I learned something. I made modifications. Looking back, I believe my journey to greatness didn't begin with my first kick—it began with the first time I dropped the ball and picked it up again.

Picking up the ball means to

- take action consistently—no matter what;
- continue to pursue greatness—no matter what; and
- never give up—no matter what.

What would be possible for you personally if, from here forward, you embraced every opportunity to pick up the ball? What would be possible for your team at work, your family, or any other aspect of your life if everyone made picking up the ball habitual? Isn't it exciting to think you can contribute to someone else's success by modeling and encouraging this tenacity?

It's also important to understand this is about more than just trying new things or doing things that scare you. It's about staying committed over time to a process and to people, regardless of temporary frustration, discomfort, or uncertainty. And it's about never giving up in spite of challenges along the way. Never giving up no matter how many times you (or someone else) may temporarily drop the ball. This is about accessing that place in your thoughts where limitless opportunities await. How many times will you ask *what else is possible* and approach that big client for the win? How many times will you ask your uncommunicative teenager about his day? How many times will you apologize or forgive and move on?

Picking up the ball gives you freedom to reach unimaginable levels of success. Picking up the ball reignites momentum, resets your confidence, and moves you one step closer to breakthrough. It encourages peak performance, greater purpose, improved mental health, and efficient teamwork. Those who always pick up the ball, and who encourage others to do the same, are the ones who truly defy limits. One bounce or bounce-back at a time. One mistake at a time. One refinement at a time. One victory at a time.

Picking up the ball is a lifestyle. There's always a fresh business strategy to implement, an upcoming certification to obtain, a new piece of technology to master. Sometimes you feel stuck and are not sure how to move forward. Reach out for help. Keep going. Picking up the ball begins with the conviction that dropping the ball is no longer the end of the story. In fact, it's the beginning of a better one—if you're willing to adjust and try again. Because the truth is, dropping the ball gives you the opportunity to pick it back up and develop inner strength and resilience. It's what allows you to work effectively as a team, to feel great at work and at home, and to strive toward a shared vision.

So—what's your vision?

What else is possible?

CHAPTER TWO

A Seemingly Impossible Goal

ANOTHER LIFE-SHAPING IDEA my young self discovered as I set and met soccer juggling and freestyle goals was a concept many people call a stretch goal, or the term I prefer, *seemingly impossible goal*. This is a measurable, next-level aspiration that pushes your limits, tests your abilities, and strengthens your determination. It breaks down your innate instinct to stay the same. It inspires collaboration, innovation, change, and focus. It's a lofty vision that might have you saying both "Can I really achieve that?" and "Maybe I could." Despite doubts, the allure of accomplishment stretches you to move forward with optimism and perseverance. And don't overlook the word *measurable*. A seemingly impossible goal must be something concrete. You will know without a doubt when you have achieved it. It must be more specifically defined than "Become a better project manager" or "Be a stronger leader." Examples of measurable goals are "Run a marathon in under four and a half hours by this time next year" or "Publish my mystery novel by the end of the summer."

Clarity fuels progress. The more specific your goal, the more achievable it becomes.

What would a seemingly impossible goal look like in your life?

First, take just a beat and think about something you would love to achieve. Go ahead and stop reading for a minute and really come up with something.

Got it? Say it in your head or out loud if you're able to. Now, if your conclusion is, "Yeah, I can do this," then your goal isn't big enough. If you are totally certain of success, it's not seemingly impossible. If you share your vision with people who know you well and they don't say something along the lines of, "That's insane," it's only hard. Go bigger than hard. How can you modify that goal to make it seemingly impossible?

A great place to start with this is by using what I call "words of elevation."

Words of Elevation

Imagine you're leading a team in your business or other organization, and you want to clarify and level up a seemingly impossible goal for your group. A great idea. To help you with this, below is a list of words and phrases that can take almost any ordinary team goal to seemingly impossible status easily and immediately:

- always
- all
- never stop
- no matter what
- even greater
- every day
- every single
- consistently
- like you've never imagined
- like never before
- exceptional

To see how you can utilize these words and phrases to make your team goal seemingly impossible, below are some examples

I've used for specific organizations in my keynote presentations to get attendees pumped up about what they want to achieve. The leadership teams and I brainstormed exactly how to word these goals to make sure they would resonate with each attendee and help push them past their previous perceived limitations. Each example includes what the ordinary goal could have looked like, followed by use of the words above to transform the goal into something seemingly impossible.

IMPROVING THE LIVES OF YOUR MEMBERS becomes:
Consistently improving the lives of your members **no matter what** challenges arise.

PROVIDING GREAT SERVICE becomes:
Always providing **world-class** service so that you **never stop** exceeding your customers' expectations.

PROVIDE EACH CITIZEN WITH OPPORTUNITIES AND FACILITIES TO ACHIEVE their **HEALTH GOALS** becomes:
Consistently provide **every** citizen with **abundant** opportunities and facilities to achieve their **seemingly impossible** health goals.

BUILD UP BETTER LEADERS IN OUR ORGANIZATION becomes:
To ensure **all of** our leaders are **always** growing and learning so they can **consistently** lead and encourage others through **any** challenge.

The addition of these descriptive words is more than just a fun exercise. They elevate the goal beyond the ordinary. Those simple additions bring vague goals into focus. They make things specific. For example, when you add "any" to "challenge," you will start thinking about and planning for bigger things. "Any" challenge includes more than just a new hire or a cyber incident. Those who have big-picture goals are infinitely more prepared for any previously inconceivable crisis. Likewise, if you are providing "abundant" opportunities for members of the community you serve to grow and succeed, you will ask *what else is possible* and seek out a solution. One in which each and every citizen—including those with unique challenges—has the opportunity to thrive in ways they never have before.

Now, remember that seemingly impossible goals are measurable. If you want to write and publish a curriculum, there is an endpoint when you hold the book in your hands. However, as evidenced by the organizational examples I've shared, some goals take more work than others to make them measurable. This means that measuring terms like "consistently" and "best" will require some creativity. Perhaps you must create the measuring tool: compiling staff surveys every quarter or once a year, calling monthly meetings to discuss employee satisfaction, sending email requests for customer reviews.

Finally, and this goes for individual as well as group goals, you must also be sure the goal is not *absolutely impossible*. If I had told my dad I wanted to juggle the soccer ball 1,000 times, barefoot on broken glass while being attacked by polar bears, he may have just stared at me. *Absolutely* means completely and totally. Juggling a soccer ball barefoot on broken glass while being attacked by polar bears wasn't in the realm of possibility for me because that He-Man thing never kicked in (dang it!). Why invest time on absolutely impossible goals when there are so many seemingly impossible goals to be conquered? *Seemingly* means outwardly or apparently. It merely *seemed* to my dad that I would never make 1,000 kicks without dropping the ball (and I'm glad I proved him wrong!).

Achieving Next-Level Greatness as a Team

The ball you are picking up is often not just yours. Picking up the ball can and should be relational. Oftentimes, low bandwidth, lack of expertise, and other challenges can make the ball too heavy for one person to lift. If you are a member of a sports team, community group, or family, here's what picking up the ball may look like on an organizational level:

- **ARE YOU FOCUSED ON THE GROUP PURPOSE?** Picture that field of seven-year-olds kicking soccer balls around. It was total chaos. We didn't even think of picking up someone else's ball because we were too focused on our own. This is amusing when it's a bunch of sweaty boys, but as responsible adults, we have to do more than watch others flail around. Why does this organism you call your business/association/organization/family exist? Do you have a common goal or mission statement? If not, maybe it's time to come up with one and make sure it's clearly communicated.

- **ARE YOU WILLING TO ASK FOR HELP?** We hear a lot about the "culture" of certain organizations. Every group has one. Does yours nurture a culture of supporting others? You may not be comfortable asking for help, but everyone benefits when you can shout out a request for support before the ball rolls out into the street and gets run over and ruined. It's your choice to avoid letting self-sufficient pride create a situation that could be easily remedied with a little assistance.

- **ARE YOU WILLING TO HELP OTHERS?** Sometimes you are picking up a ball for a teammate. Just imagine—a coworker makes a mistake, and instead of blaming them (easy to do but not generally productive) you come alongside to look for solutions. How about the next time you are frustrated with someone's error and have the impulse to complain or gossip, pick up the ball and bring your challenge to them directly.

In order to always be growing as one team, everyone must be committed to the bigger goal, constantly communicating, and consistently engaged.

Remember how I have eight daughters? My days are full. It took a few years into my entrepreneurial journey to recognize my need for assistance with daily tasks. But after reading Dan Sullivan and Dr. Benjamin Hardy's book, *Who Not How: The Formula to Achieve Bigger Goals Through Accelerating Teamwork*, I came to the realization that I was overwhelmed by *how*—how I would build a website, how I would publicize my keynotes, how I would make more time to spend with family. That's when I realized the focus shouldn't be on *how*, but rather, *who*. Who could I find to help with this overwhelming list of tasks? Whose expertise could I tap into to break new ground with my business? Who could I hire to free up more minutes in my day to spend time with my daughters? In order to bring you my keynotes and even this book, I finally realized I had to hire some support. That's when I started building a team to handle parts of the business I wasn't great at or didn't enjoy doing, which enabled me to focus on my creativity, my zone of genius, and my audiences.

I have been greatly inspired by another one of Dan Sullivan and Dr. Benjamin Hardy's books, *10x is Easier Than 2x: How World-Class Entrepreneurs Achieve More by Doing Less*. Their premise is that in order to double your business, you have to work twice as hard as you are now. For me that would mean doubling office hours, doubling meeting times, and doubling days on the road. The thought of ramping up like that is paralyzing. But they say the possibility of creating a business that's ten times more than it is today is something to get excited about. When you look at *ten times* more, you start to create these seemingly impossible goals. You begin to let go of the things that are not important. Do I really need to proofread and approve every social media post my coordinator creates? Probably not. I let that go, and even though there might be a typo in some video subtitles once in a while, I now have another half hour plus to spend on things which better align with my values. When you ask *who* rather than *how* you can let go of eighty percent of the work you don't have the skills or desire to accomplish. You can ask someone else to do it or simply drop it all together. True progress isn't about pure grind, it's about reaching the finish line with your health, integrity, and family intact.

Today I have an executive assistant, a coach, a bookkeeper, a tax person, a webmaster, a podcast production and marketing team, a social media coordinator, and an editor, just to name a few. I even pay someone to mow my lawn. When I started working with a team, I gained significant traction in my career and freed up my time and mind space to focus more on important things like my family. The only challenge was finding the right people, but once I did, countless opportunities began to open up for my professional and personal life. It was sometimes a scary move to hand those tasks off to others, but surrounding myself with specialists who know more than I do in certain areas is the smartest thing I could have done. Assembling this talented group has fueled my entrepreneurial spirit and freed me up to focus on what I'm passionate about—encouraging and inspiring you.

What's weighing on you today? What tasks are draining your time and pulling you away from what truly matters? If your vision board is starting to feel like a distant dream, maybe it's time to think even bigger. Instead of asking, "How will I get through this?" start asking, "Who can help?" Shifting your mindset can turn those overwhelming goals back into achievable realities.

Risking It for the Reward

Oftentimes business can be a lot like soccer freestyle. Every daring, seemingly impossible new trick comes with risks. You can keep it safe and just do more moderate moves if you choose to, but the bigger the trick, the more danger involved. One time I was attempting a freestyle "half around the world–around the world" combo move. It's a trick where I kick the ball and, in the same motion, my foot rotates around it and quickly comes back down so the other foot can finish the move. However, my foot landed on the ball, went sideways, and I broke a bone in my foot. Temporarily dropping the ball (maybe even breaking the proverbial foot), is an unavoidable and necessary part of the road to distinction. That means imperfection, vulnerability, and humility all come as part of the deal.

Despite the risks associated with freestyle, the fact that it makes soccer juggling more fun, more rewarding, and more challenging makes it all worthwhile. It constantly drives me to a next level of greatness and keeps me asking, *What else is possible*? It also made me realize this: Everyone has their own soccer freestyle equivalent—that thing that tests you, that pushes you, that would be so beautiful if you could pull it off. What does next level greatness look like for you? What's *your* "soccer freestyle?" What thing would you like to create for yourself this week? This month? This year? In your lifetime? What seemingly impossible goal is in your sight? What risks are you willing to take to reap greater rewards?

And . . . what mindset does it take, exactly, to inspire, energize, and create something that's truly next level?

What else is possible?

CHAPTER THREE

The Possibility Mindset

HOW WOULD YOU describe the words "possible" or "possibility"? We use them so frequently they have almost become cliches, particularly when it comes to goal setting. If one of my younger kids asked me out of the blue what "possibility" means, I wonder if I might have a hard time fully explaining the term. I know what it means and how to use it in a sentence. I can see the outline and subtle shading of the word, but finding other words to add color to the picture becomes a challenge.

So, when you initially hear me use the term "possibility mindset," maybe you'll be able to see the outline of the amazing things to come, but it will take some tools and guidance to color in the picture. Consider this your art class. And like art, some people find this process comes more naturally, where others may have to work a little harder at it.

For as long as I can remember, I have instinctively lived with what I now call the possibility mindset. It is just innate in me. You could say I was born with it. I am tenacious, and no matter what others say, I hear, "Go get it! Don't quit!" It has always been a part of who I am. I honestly didn't know what to call it for a long time. Even as a kid I had a drive to always try new things and knew if I worked hard enough, I would achieve mastery over them. Piano, guitar, drums, soccer, baseball—if there was a new skill to be learned, I was all over it. Even today I would love to learn how to play the bagpipes, but I have to balance that with my desire to watch my kids grow up. So, whether you were born with the possibility mindset or you need to learn it, either way you can embrace it more and more with each thought.

Embracing the possibility mindset goes hand in hand with embracing failure as a means for growth and learning. When I first set out to support myself by performing magic, I walked into forty restaurants looking for work as a tableside magician. I landed just two of them. That's thirty-eight fails. But you know what? That process is what started my career. Those two gigs paid off a little college debt and helped me keep asking, *What else is possible?*

Even basketball great Michael Jordan lost almost three hundred games, but we remember him for his wins. He said, "I've failed over and over and over again in my life. And that is why I succeed." It's like failing your way forward. That's how you win. As a quote attributed to Dale Carnegie goes, "Discouragement and failure are two of the surest stepping stones to success."

What bothers me more than mere failure is the temptation to give up. I remember learning a playing card move where you spread the cards on your forearm all the way from your wrist to your elbow, then throw them up in the air and catch them. I started by holding my arm over the bed because, hey, I knew the cards would keep falling and it's not so far to bend over and pick them up off the bed rather than the floor. I expected to fail for a while. I picked the cards up again and again. But I didn't give up, and eventually I was able to wow audiences with that showy maneuver—minus the bed, of course (that would've been weird).

This doesn't necessarily mean you always *plan* to fail; you just don't let the fear of failure hold you back. And as long as you don't allow setbacks to become endings, you are beginning to embrace the possibility mindset.

Believe me (or just ask my family) when I say I am not always a super jovial individual. I regularly struggle with staying positive. I get it. I have identified a lot of negativity in myself that I've had to (and still have to) overcome. But that gives me a unique perspective to help others recognize and eradicate it from their own thinking. I love to encourage people and help them see the good in themselves. I know how much I need affirmation, whether it's feedback after I speak to an audience or just the fact someone noticed my new shirt. So I'm here now to affirm you and, most importantly, to teach you to affirm yourself. This positive energy can be the fuel you need to take that next leap forward.

Here's some good news: You don't have to make a total transformation overnight. Success—whether in small wins or major breakthroughs—is a step-by-step process.

Take my experience with soccer juggling, for example. By setting regular milestones and celebrating each one, I turned what once seemed impossible into reality. This approach—breaking big ambitions into smaller, achievable steps—is known as "proximal goals," a principle backed by behavioral psychology for over a century.

Even today, the most successful individuals and teams share a common trait: They balance a bold vision with incremental goals. This combination is one factor that sets high achievers apart from the rest. And when challenges arise, the possibility mindset becomes one of your greatest allies. Instead of letting fear or uncertainty hold you back, ask yourself, *What else is possible*? That simple shift in perspective can expand both your vision and your results.

AS LONG AS YOU DON'T ALLOW SETBACKS TO BECOME ENDINGS, YOU ARE BEGINNING TO EMBRACE THE POSSIBILITY MINDSET

Harnessing Your Vision

With few exceptions, great accomplishments begin as a vision. A dream. A stretch. The first step to feed potential and starve limitation is to hold a vision in your mind. But not just any vision—your seemingly impossible goal. Studies have shown that people and organizations who visualize a stretch goal can pioneer new ideas and major strides in innovation, productivity, and impact. For example, 3M has long embraced the "15 percent culture" that allows employees to spend 15 percent of their work time pursuing innovative passion projects. This mindset was born when 3M was a small sandpaper manufacturer with an aspiring young engineer named Richard G. Drew. Drew invented Scotch tape on his own time, and that kept the company afloat during the Great Depression, when "Make do and mend" was the slogan of the day.

It's highly likely your favorite sports, music, or pop culture heroes use visualization as a path to success. I live in Kansas City, so I have to use a Chiefs example in my book—it's sort of a rule we have here. Chiefs placekicker Harrison Butker, who so far has helped the team clinch three Super Bowls, has gone on record many times about the importance of seeing a successful field goal in his mind before his foot meets the ball. Butker physically trains and works hard and does everything in his power to help make that seemingly impossible game-winning field goal happen, but the mental game is key.

And now it's time for another magic trick. I believe one of the reasons so many people love magic is because of how it appears to defy the impossible. It creates anticipation, engagement, and fun, and it's one of my best training tools. The metaphors and life applications are plentiful and powerful, and one of the illusions I use in my keynotes helps audience members create a collective vision for their organization. This works for businesses, professional associations, and community and faith groups, just to name a few. Let's try it here.

First, we focus on four pivotal questions. In my keynotes, I randomly choose four participants to answer them—but here, *you* get to answer all of them. Slow down and take a minute to come up with an answer for each question. Feel free to write in the book (unless you borrowed it)!

QUESTION 1:

- Pursuing greater possibilities is often about external factors, but sometimes it's about how you *choose to feel* about your reality. Imagine feeling more centered during imperfect situations, or even during the times that test you most. If anything were possible, what emotion would you love to *always* feel when you are at work or with your community group? Successful, creative, energetic, and confident are some common responses I receive during my keynotes. Love, joy, peace, and patience are other possibilities. Positive emotions like these contribute to a positive team culture, foster cooperation, and enhance overall performance. Which one positive emotion resonates with you right now? Which would you *always* love to feel?

QUESTION 2:

- Now think of your organization's key values. Integrity, innovation, teamwork, excellence, and transparency are a few of the principles practiced by some of the highest-performing organizations in the world (if it's more applicable to you, just think of the value most important in your life). Which value would you love to experience most fully *every day*?

QUESTION 3:

- Who in your organization (or your life) has made a positive impact on you (name just one person)?

QUESTION 4:

- Here's an off-the-wall one: Which celebrity are you a huge fan of, living or dead?

Be sure to pay attention to these italicized words in the first two questions: *always* and *every day*. I'm not asking about generalizations, but specific, repeatable emotions and values. This sets the bar higher for the successful outcome of both your mindset shift and my illusion.

Let's say the emotion you would like to *always* experience at work is confidence. You struggle with self-doubt and wonder if people are talking about you behind your back. Now if your answer to the second question about key value—the virtue you would like to embody every day—is integrity, how does that tie in? Try stepping outside of the situation and looking at your interactions with team members. Do you operate with integrity—telling the truth, encouraging without flattery, and keeping their best interests in mind? If you do, the only gossip you're likely to overhear is how awesome you are. Often you will see the application of a positive value such as integrity will shore up those elusive energizing emotions such as confidence.

And do you have your answers for questions three and four— did you think of a person who has made an impact on you and did you choose a favorite celebrity? Now remember, at my keynotes, four different audience members answer each question. I ask one random person to share a positive emotion, another to mention a key value, another to describe someone who has made an impact on them, and one to name a celebrity. This is so random, in fact, that I choose participants by throwing out a beach ball into the audience. Whoever catches the ball answers one question and then tosses it to someone else. There's no way I could know who would catch it or what they might say.

But here's where the real fun starts: A week or so before the gig, I FedEx the event planner a big envelope with strict instructions to keep it sealed. I call it the "Envelope of Mystery." Of course, by the time I arrive the event planner is dying to know what's inside. Finally, in my keynote, after we have discussed those four audience members' answers, I call the event planner up front with the envelope. I still haven't touched it. They tear it open and inside is another sealed envelope, and inside that are two index cards sealed with a ring of staples. When they tear apart the stapled cards, there's a note inside that reveals the *exact words and names* chosen at random by the audience in the minutes prior. Yes, even the exact name of the impactful person! At this point the audience is freaked out—rightfully so.

So, how could I have possibly predicted a week beforehand what arbitrary audience members were going to say? Can you keep a secret? So can I. Come on, you know the rule—magicians don't share secrets of the trade. But I *will* reveal how the use of illusion creates an atmosphere where new ideas and dreams are planted and begin to take root.

When the event planner reads the prediction, audiences are always amazed, but more importantly, they are engaged in new possibilities for their group. They have created a seemingly impossible goal. More than just a list, the words I wrote days before are in a narrative designed to pull them all together.

This is the story they hear that I have written down and sealed securely in the envelope days prior to the event. Please read it by inserting your own answers to the four pivotal questions: "Last night I dreamed I was speaking to an incredible group of people. In my dream, they created a seemingly impossible goal together, where *every day*, people feel (your emotion) and *always* grow a culture of (your value). They all make an impact like (person who has made an impact on you), and create loyal fans like (your celebrity)."

Oh . . . did you think *your* randomly chosen words were actually going to be written in this book? Sorry if I misled you, but come on—I'm not Criss Angel.

So just imagine deeply experiencing that positive emotion every single day as you go about your life and work—while continually growing that inner value you know will bring deeper meaning to everything you do. Picture having as much influence on others as the person who has impacted you. And yes, even creating a fan-base like Chris Pratt's (had to throw in my celebrity reference): the kind of loyalty where the people you lead can't stop talking about you. You become a celebrity in your own right. Can you feel the excitement that kind of vision would spark in you each day? Imagine how much more passionately you'd show up. This is a seemingly impossible goal.

As for my keynote presentations—before the event even ends, the team becomes fully invested in that shared mental picture *together*. They begin to see what's possible: working effectively as a unit, feeling great both coming to work and going home, and striving collectively toward the vision they just *magically* created.

Here's a key takeaway from that illusion—one I always em-phasize to the audience and want *you* to hold on to: When your vision is strong enough, other people can sense it.

They want to be part of it—whether as participants or encour-agers. Imagine your vision being so strong that others can *see* it without you saying a word, like an illusionist who seems to read your thoughts.

So . . . how strong is your vision? Is it contagious enough that others catch it? Do the people around you know what you want, what you're passionate about, what you're pursuing? Try this: Ask your closest friends what they think you desire most right now. If they can answer accurately, it means you're fully invested—because your actions are speaking for you. Your behavior reflects your vision.

WHEN YOUR VISION IS STRONG ENOUGH, OTHER PEOPLE CAN SENSE IT

It will take teamwork to achieve the seemingly impossible goal you just created—whether that means colleagues at work or the support of family, friends, mentors, and others. Collaboration will amp up your creativity and push the outer limits of your potential.

At first, it might feel overwhelming. But remember: It all happens one thought, one action, and one success at a time.

Your Vision Word

Let's focus for a moment on a specific personal goal of yours. A seemingly impossible goal. It can take shape at home, at work, or somewhere in your community—every aspect of your life is game because they all interact. Anything come to mind? Here are some thoughts to get you started:

- First and most important: This goal excites you! It makes you want to take action immediately when you talk about it.
- There's a small part of you that believes you might be able to do it if you can support it with the proper conditions, but it's a stretch. It pushes you far beyond the reaches of familiar boundaries.
- It's measurable: You will know without a doubt when you get there.

Got something in mind? Now let's narrow it down even further. Label this seemingly impossible goal with one word. How hard can that be? I mean the English language only has about one hundred and seventy thousand words currently in use. My best advice is to go with your first instinct. Don't overthink it.

Why one word? Mission statements are often hard to remember because they're too wordy or overly complicated and have no emotional connection for the members. But for you, this one word is incredibly clear, easy to remember, and can't *not* connect with you emotionally.

If your goal is to start a nonprofit benefiting the underserved in the community, it might be *others*. If it's to write a book, it might be *publish*. If it's to buy a vacation home, it might be *relax* or *expensive*. You get the idea. This is your vision word.

Now, one thing I know a little about is the childbirth process. My wife doesn't need a birthing coach, aka a *doula*, because she has me, her "dude-la." One key thing midwives teach laboring moms is to visualize the end result of the pain. How are you going to feel when you hold that baby in your hands? So, let's try that here (but not with the childbirth thing; that could get out of hand real quick). Rather than visualizing the details of how you will reach your vision word, picture the outcome and how it will make you feel. What would be great about reaching that goal? What would be the *best thing* about it? Are there any things you can think of that have been holding you back up to this point? Sometimes certain life factors may threaten to destroy your vision. Other things might demand your attention. Self-doubt or negativity from others could creep in. It's up to you to keep the vision intact.

Sometimes during my keynote speeches, we hand out note-cards for audience members to record their vision words. This is important because goals require a visual. There's a whiteboard onstage. I write a word on it, but the audience can't see what it is since the board is facing away from them. Then I call someone up on the other end of the stage where a newspaper is laid out. There are easily tens of thousands of words in the newspaper. I ask the volunteer to choose one word from those thousands and say it out loud. They do so, and then comes the big reveal—I spin the board around and everyone can see I had written the same word my volunteer just chose! Sometimes audiences clap; sometimes they are too shocked and just sit with their mouths open. But that's just the warm-up for the next part. It then becomes time to amplify the amazing factor and the significance of this routine.

While everyone is still in awe and I'm still at the other end of the stage, I turn the whiteboard away from the audience once again and write down another word. I then ask the volunteer to say what their vision word is and immediately turn the board around to reveal I correctly predicted their word! Think you know how it's done? Me neither—I've been trying to figure out how I do it for years.

All of the fun of this routine is to help hit home the fact that your vision word acts like a "magic word" in your mind. Studies show you are more likely to experience success with the goal your vision word represents because you have a picture of it in your mind's eye. Perhaps those vision boards we see all over social media really do make an impact. But are you skeptical of the psychology of creating positive outcomes through focused thought? If so, at least consider that no outcomes will exist until you first have an idea. Nearly every tool, belief, or breakthrough began as a single thought—an idea someone dared to explore.

The Blessing of a Shared Vision

I remember I was absolutely certain I would know who I would marry by the time I graduated from college. When that didn't happen, I started thinking, *Will I ever get married?* On some level, it started to begin to feel impossible, but I really wanted to get married. So, my vision word could have been *ball*, or *chain* (just another joke from the keynote). Doubts and fears crept into my head. Would I ever find the right person? Could I feel confident making that big of a decision? I was definitely overthinking things. Do you ever do that?

Well, I'm happy to say my wife Lynn and I are coming up on eighteen years of marriage. When we first got married, we had a unified vision. We both wanted kids, but the goal was slightly different for each of us. I was thinking two. One-to-one coverage. But she wanted to test the outer limits of possibilities, so we had the two, then three, then—as it turns out, I love having kids, so I soon changed my mind on that two-is-ideal thing. As I mentioned earlier, we have eight girls, including one that was born while I was writing this book. It's what we do.

With this many kids, you have to maintain a sense of humor. Before my wife's most recent pregnancy, people would ask me, "You trying for that boy?"

I would just point to my bounty of beautiful girls and say, "Do we look like quitters? No. We're overachievers."

Sometimes people say, "It's a bummer you don't have boys— have you thought about adoption?" I just jokingly respond, "Yeah we thought about it, then we were like, 'Ah never mind, we'll just keep 'em.'"

The Henderson sorority all started with my seemingly impossible goal of wanting to get married. Then, Lynn and I started small with our family, bringing souls into the world one at a time. We both envisioned a family, but what we have now is a more beautiful picture than either one of us could have dreamed. That's the great thing about vision, and especially a shared one; it often turns out better and richer than you first imagined.

Throwing Off Every Hindrance

As I mentioned earlier, pursuing a vision isn't just about working harder or piling more onto your plate. In fact, sometimes the key to unlocking your next level of greatness isn't in what you add—it's in what you let go of. We often hold onto things we believe we need, unaware that they might actually be weighing us down. But what if releasing them is the very thing that propels us forward? Let me show you what I mean—with a little magic.

Have you ever heard of David Blaine? He's that street magician who's famously unsettling—in the best way. He'll walk up to strangers and say, "Hey, can I show you something?" and they'd say, "Nah, we're good." Then, two seconds later, he's melted their brains, and they're ready to be best friends for life. The man wins people over fast.

When I was eighteen, David Blaine opened my eyes to what else was possible. In my keynote, I perform a trick inspired by one I saw him do on TV—a routine with cards and coins designed to spark that same sense of wonder in my audience. Here's how it works:

I lay out four coins in a square on the table, covering each one with a playing card. Then, one by one, I remove the cards—only to reveal that the coins have "invisibly" traveled, all gathering under a single card. It's a fun trick to perform, and for a long time, I believed the cards were absolutely necessary. I mean, logically, how else could the trick work? The cards provide the cover that makes the magic possible.

Or so I thought.

This is where we get trapped: believing something is *essential* when, in reality, it's the very thing limiting us. Maybe you've had a great idea but instantly dismissed it as impossible. *Nope, can't happen.* Logic convinces us to stay inside the lines, to stick with what we know. But what if we didn't? What if we questioned the rules we assume are unbreakable?

That's exactly what magician John B. Born did. He applied the possibility mindset and asked *What if this trick could be done without the cards?* At first, it seemed absurd—after all, the cards were the secret to making the coins travel. But he persisted. And in doing so, John didn't just perform the trick without the cards—he elevated it. Without the limitations of the cards, new possibilities opened up, allowing for even greater breakthroughs.

Maybe you've experienced something similar. Maybe the thing you think you *need*—even if it's a good thing—is actually keeping you from your full potential. The moment you find the courage to let go, the results may surprise you. The sky becomes the limit when you stop holding on to the things that keep you grounded.

At this point in my keynote, I perform the trick again, this time without the playing cards. And just like that, the coins move, defying logic even more than before. The effect is stronger. The illusion is more powerful. And all because someone let go of what he once thought was necessary.

As I conclude, I hold up the cards and toss them aside, one by one as I say:

- "Sometimes, greater possibilities start with getting rid of the cards." (*toss*)
- "What you think is helping you might actually be holding you back." (*toss*)
- "What's in your way?" (*toss*)
- "What do you need to let go of? What hindrance, what addiction, what time-consuming habit is keeping you from a significant breakthrough?" (*toss*)

So, what cards are in your hand? And are you ready to let them go?

What else is possible?

CHAPTER FOUR

My Magical Journey

LET'S START THIS chapter with a fun question: What do my sister's friend Kelly, Joey McIntyre from New Kids on the Block, and magician David Blaine all have in common? Well, unless you're my mom or my sister you'll never guess, so I'll go ahead and tell you. They are just a few of the surprisingly large number of people who inspired me to pursue a career in magic, which has fed directly into and given me lots of material for my passion of motivational speaking. Thinking back on my life, I've been reminded that when you latch onto the greatness of others, it helps you see the potential for greatness in yourself.

This chapter is about my journey, but as you read it, I want you to think about yourself. How did you get from point A to point B and all the way to your current situation? Maybe you've seen the "how it started—how it's going" posts online. What would yours look like if you could go back to that time when you were still trying to bring your future into focus? What kind of pictures were flashing through your mind? Take a second and think about experiences you've had, people you've met along the way, and how all of that prepared you for the path you are walking today.

WHEN YOU LATCH ONTO THE GREATNESS OF OTHERS, IT HELPS YOU SEE THE POTENTIAL FOR GREATNESS IN YOURSELF

Early Exposure to Magic

Back in second grade, my sister's friend Kelly amazed me with some magic I'll never forget. Gretchen, my sister, is two years older than me, and like a good younger brother, I took every chance I could to infiltrate her social circle. One evening when Gretchen had Kelly over for a sleepover, she did a coin trick and two card tricks for us. I'll never forget those simple tricks and the feeling of wonder they created in me. The best part of that night was that after wowing us with her magic, she thankfully broke the magician's code and revealed the secrets behind those tricks. *You mean I can do this too?* I couldn't believe it. Like most good illusions, pulling them off was harder than it looked, but with a little practice I could perform them effectively. (Along with the magic tricks, Kelly also taught me how to launch spit bubbles from my mouth and watch them float to the floor, but that isn't connected to the magic, so forget I mentioned it.)

There were other brief moments of magic that came my way growing up. One time, my friend's brother did a trick where he made a ball disappear from a small vase. He put the ball in, covered it with the lid, and *bam*, it was gone. It was amazing. Another time, years before the Kelly sleepover, a magician performing at our grocery store (I know, cool grocery store!) did the zig-zag illusion with a playing card, meaning he apparently split the card into three parts and then incredibly put the pieces back together. And I was thinking, *How did he do that?* I was right there, and he did it two feet from my face. It was close up, not on a big stage where he could have fooled us with smoke and mirrors and—oops, forgot I'm not supposed to reveal any secrets of magic. It didn't occur to me that I could pull off something like the zig-zag illusion. That early on, the thought of becoming a professional magician had not even entered my mind. Yet each one of these experiences was a stepping stone that built my interest and brought me closer and closer to realizing the magical possibilities ahead of me.

Then there were the superstars like David Copperfield, who made the Statue of Liberty disappear, and David Blaine, who introduced me to the concept of street magic. For a long time, I assumed you had to be a special person to execute these incredible feats. Not a wizard or anything like that, but just someone with unique talents. Someone famous, with the ability and resources to do big things in front of big audiences or on TV. I figured only certain people were cut out for that life—I had no idea how huge and diverse the world of magic and illusion really was.

The Joey Trick

One day, Gretchen brought home a New Kids on the Block VHS tape. (If you're not familiar with NKOTB, think Jackson 5, Backstreet Boys, One Direction, or any boy band of your era.) Gretchen was a big fan of the New Kids, so by default, I was too. At that time, it was not popular to be a boy and like that group, so I was a closet fan. Then I watched Gretchen's new VHS tape and became an even bigger fan, but still closet. The video included some candid backstage footage where Joey McIntyre (my sister's favorite) showed his hands completely empty, then did the classic trick of pulling a series of colorful silk handkerchiefs from his closed fist. He was pretty cool to me already, but after seeing that trick, he instantly became my favorite (sorry, Donnie). I seriously wondered if it was a camera trick, so I rewound and watched the clip many times because I wanted to know how he did it—I wanted to learn the Joey trick. Even after a lot of slow motion and pausing I *still* couldn't figure it out. (Fun side note: In case you don't know, NKOTB has made a comeback, and as I write this, my sister is at their concert here in KC.)

Incidentally, not long after I first saw that clip, the late Kansas

City magician L. C. Collier put on a magic show at one of our school assemblies at Broken Arrow Elementary when I was in fifth grade. L. C. called for a volunteer, and next thing I knew I found myself on stage and involved in one of his illusions. It was super exciting being up in front of people, getting that attention. It almost felt like I was the magician. It only made the intrigue and desire to learn magic tricks that much stronger, and it was a pivotal moment where I envisioned myself performing in front of people for the very first time. This was when that powerful little *seemingly impossible goal* took root in my spirit. I made a tiny jump toward my future that day. And you'll never guess what trick L. C. performed—the Joey trick! I couldn't believe it. It *wasn't* a camera trick. So I decided right then I *must* learn the Joey trick.

I figured there might be books on how to do magic tricks (this was pre-Internet), so I asked my mom to drive me to the library. A special shout-out to my mom here. She always supported my attempts to learn anything, whether it was soccer or piano or magic, and now that I'm a parent myself I realize she consistently made sacrifices so I could pursue that next big thing. And shout-out to my dad as well, God rest his soul, who built some props and rigged up several magic gimmicks for me growing up. My parents were the best—they were an integral part of me living my dream.

That evening, my mom *did* drive me to the library, and I checked out about a dozen books on magic, hoping to discover the secret to the Joey trick. I didn't even care about other magic tricks, just that one illusion. I did find one way to make a handkerchief disappear, but it was obvious to me it wasn't the same method Joey and L. C. used. My friends and even some of their parents tried to help me figure it out. During this time of research and reading I discovered that you don't have to be famous to be a magician. There are birthday party magicians and magicians on cruise ships and college campuses. Magicians perform in restaurants and on small stages all over the world.

Eventually, I talked to the right people and learned that you can't do the Joey trick without the right kind of special magic equipment. I needed some authentic props and gimmicks. So I went to the Yellow Pages (I'm really dating myself here), found there was a local magic shop at the rear of U. S. Toy, a giant toy store and teacher supply warehouse, and purchased everything I needed to become Joey McIntyre (mostly). I started practicing, and "Step by Step," by "Hangin' Tough," I learned "The Right Stuff" (those references were for you New Kids fans).

Through that whole process, something interesting happened. As I was investigating how to do the Joey Trick and looking through endless magic books, every once in a while I would get "distracted" with other tricks. There were tricks involving coins, playing cards, and rope. I had been slowly picking up on the art of magic in general and went back and mastered more illusions beyond the Joey trick. And that's one of the beauties of committing to learning new things—many times it will expand your world beyond what you had originally planned. That's why I am a big believer in active growing and learning, because it opens your world to endless possibilities.

One of the tricks I learned from the library books was a rubber band trick. My friends and family would watch me make a rubber band disappear and ask, "Where'd it *go*?" "How'd you *do* that?" Those reactions were music to my ears, and I began falling in love with creating those experiences for people. It was really fun to fool them. My sister even asked if part of my obsession with the art had to do with enjoying knowing something other people didn't know. That may have been a small part of it, but it wasn't what drove me. It was mainly about what I could create.

Sidenote to you would-be magicians: One piece of advice I can give is to expect to get "busted" on a trick from time to time.

As I was practicing on family and friends, they would say, "Oh, I saw that," or "I know how you did that," and it would crush me. After working for hours to fool people, I felt like a failure when the secrets were exposed. That's part of the process of what it takes to become a magician—but, like any endeavor, you just pick up the ball and keep going.

Fast-forward to my middle school and high school years and—believe it or not—my focus wandered. My friends didn't even know me as the magic guy, even though once in a while I'd have a deck of cards on me. The next big magic moment for me came at the end of high school when David Blaine, who I apparently can't stop talking about, hit the streets and my TV screen. In contrast to David Copperfield, who was doing huge illusions with animals and motorcycles and train cars, David Blaine was doing tricks in people's hands that were way beyond anything I could imagine possible. In fact, for a long time I was convinced he had plants wandering the streets to help him pull off these things on camera. There was simply no other explanation, was there? This lured me back into magic, and as I began to study more and more, I developed enough base information to figure out most of Blaine's tricks. Then, I went to a youth retreat and met a guy who was also a David Blaine fan and way more advanced in his knowledge and willing to share it with me. That got me really fired up.

You see what was happening throughout my early years, right? My journey toward becoming a professional magician was one inspiring springboard after the next.

It *Is* a Wonderful Life

This is a fun trip down memory lane for me, but what about you? What are some childhood memories you have that helped reveal your skills, talents, and interests? The plot of *It's a Wonderful Life* really does ring true when you think of how different life might be today if you hadn't spent time with certain key people at pivotal times in your childhood or young adulthood. It's amazing to think of what my girls might end up doing with their lives. As each day passes, their individual personalities evolve, and the picture of each of their futures begins to take shape. It's my job to encourage and nurture their interests and provide resources for them to explore where life may take them. I relish that role, and I am fully aware that it is accompanied by great responsibility.

Our oldest daughter, Claire, is a force of nature. She is uniquely gifted with all the firstborn characteristics, and her mom and I have watched her rise to leadership positions everywhere she goes. Claire's first job was in fast food. Not just any fast food, but a chain known for its family-centric, friendly atmosphere: Chick-fil-A. Claire worked at Chick-fil-A Lenexa, owned and operated by Drew Severns, who is an incredible leader and has developed a team of uniquely exceptional individuals. (Fun fact: Drew's brother Will Severns is the cofounder of Streamline, the publisher of this book.) Drew and his leadership team have created a restaurant where young teens and even those with special needs are given real responsibility and training in serving others. They help employees see that work is more than earning gas money; more than the paycheck at the end of the month. I am certain their investment of time and generosity with their wisdom made a tremendous impact on Claire's future. After she resigned from nearly three years with the restaurant, Drew sent her an email affirming her contributions and sending her on her way with a blessing. It was a meaningful letter that brought Claire, her mother, and me to tears.

Who in your life needs that encouragement, nurturing, or full-on mentoring? Is there a younger person you could take out for coffee just to listen to them dream out loud? Is there someone at work or in your friend group who seems to be struggling and in need of your wisdom and care? Consider what might happen if you made an effort to help a new teammate at work get acclimated. Not only could you create a more welcoming, productive atmosphere for them, but you would also reap the benefits of positivity and forward movement yourself.

Several years ago, a promising young teenager named Grant—an aspiring magician—reached out to me for advice. A few years later, after starting college and opening up to his parents about what he really wanted in life, his dad gave me a call and asked, "Is Grant's dream of becoming a professional magician actually realistic?"

His dad's hesitation was completely understandable. Could this really be a career? Could it actually work? I told him yes—I believed it could. Grant had the personality, the passion, and the raw skill to give it a real shot. And guess what? He did it. He became a full-time magician. Today, he's supporting his wife and kids—and he's thriving. It means the world to know that just as others once inspired me, I had the chance to inspire him. One of life's greatest rewards is helping someone step into their next seemingly impossible goal.

To University and Beyond

The next phase of my journey with magic was after I graduated from high school and enrolled at Johnson County Community College here in Kansas. Once the semester began, I started carrying coins and cards everywhere I went, quickly becoming the community college's version of David Blaine. I quickly became "the magic guy." I even learned how to "steal" watches like David Blaine, practicing in this low-stakes situation with people on campus. If someone caught on and realized I was trying to pick-pocket their watch in the process of a coin trick, I figured I was much less likely to get accused of actually trying to steal on a college campus than if I were honing this skill on the streets of

ONE OF LIFE'S GREATEST REWARDS IS HELPING SOMEONE STEP INTO THEIR NEXT SEEMINGLY IMPOSSIBLE GOAL

New York. I would simply explain myself, laugh it off, and move on to the next unexpecting victim. I was building my craft, and it was really, really fun. At this point I landed my first paid gig at the college employee picnic. Doing what I love for money? I was ecstatic. My mom worked at the college and got me connected with the right people—thanks, Mom! Yet again, she was propelling me toward living my dream.

My next stop was Kansas State University and a built-in audience within my fraternity (shout-out to my Lambda Chi Alpha brothers). My mom finally got a break from watching every single magic trick I was practicing. The university life provided plenty of talent shows, parties, and special events, and I started to get enough exposure to land more paid gigs. The Manhattan, Kansas, Chipotle actually hired me to do the grand opening, and my payment was in burritos. Lots of burritos. Then I became the magic *and* burrito guy, treating my friends whenever I got the chance. I did fourteen of these Chipotle appearances around Kansas, Missouri, and Nebraska over the next few years, and eventually they paid me in cash, which I'm pretty sure I spent on burritos. It's the circle of life.

Campus living also had a huge impact on the trajectory of my personal life. One fine day I met a fine young lady, a member of the Kappa Kappa Gamma sorority, on the sidewalk outside my fraternity. Long story short, I eventually married that fine lady around the same time I was beginning to pursue magic as a living. It's so cool looking back at how she was with me from the beginning. She has seen it all. This is worth mentioning here because, frankly, Lynn is always worth mentioning, and also—from the time we started dating until now, she has been the person who has given me the most inspiration and support to keep going. Even when things aren't always easy, her words, prayers, and hugs are why I am where I am today. This goes back to that whole propelling people on to their next seemingly impossible goal idea. Lynn has for sure done that for me. Her devotion as a wife and mother are proof that something greater is always possible.

I graduated from K-State with a bachelor's degree in Family Studies and Human Services and had to decide if I was going to get my master's degree and become a marriage and family therapist or go all-in with becoming a full-time magician. *Perform magic or help married people? Ahhhh—this is so hard!* People would tell me if I just made the husband disappear, I'd kind of be doing both. I graduated in December of 2003 and moved back home to give myself at least the spring and summer semesters to see if I could gain some momentum as a working magician. But where to start? I decided the answer was restaurants. I knew for a fact that some restaurants had magicians who roamed from table to table, entertaining customers as they waited for their food.

I opened up the Yellow Pages (in case you whippersnappers didn't look it up when I mentioned it earlier, the Yellow Pages is a phone book, which is a list of businesses and their phone numbers . . . wow, I just had to give the explanation an explanation), calling around to local restaurants, asking if they wanted a magician. I mean, that's not a weird phone call. *Yes, hello, you know how you serve food? You know what would make it taste better? Magic.* Those weren't my *exact* words, but I would soon realize making phone calls might be the wrong approach, because no one showed a bit of interest. On one call, I finally thought to ask who the person was who would be able to make the decision to hire a magician (as if it was in their job description). The person on the phone said it would be the GM, or general manager. So, on my calls, I started asking for the GM. They weren't always there. That wasn't helping much. Once I finally got the feeling that the phone wasn't the way to go, I realized a better approach might be to visit the restaurants in person.

Years later, I found there are communities of magicians who learn from each other, and some even have workshops on how to land gigs in restaurants. It's a whole thing, and there are techniques for effectively getting your foot in the door. I didn't know any of those tactics at the time; I just did what felt right and learned along the way. I felt as though nothing could stop me. And honestly, I'm glad I didn't know the "rules" of how to properly lay out a business proposition. Are you like me? Do you ever feel the more you try to prepare for something, the more you get into your head about how the process should look, and it thwarts your creativity and passion and spontaneity? I've known some people who feel so strongly the need to be fully prepared in their endeavors that they never take action. Sure, learning and preparation have their place in life, and I've already stated I'm a big believer in lifelong learning, but every once in a while, it's best to let your instincts be your guide and just start ugly.

I'll give you one example of just how ugly this whole process was for me. Being a family studies major, I wasn't very savvy with business jargon. When one GM asked me what I expected for compensation, I didn't know what he meant by compensation. I was thinking like worker's compensation when you get hurt—at the time I didn't realize it also meant getting paid for your time and work. So I started shooting from the hip about how I didn't anticipate getting hurt on the job and how my magic tricks are safe for spectators, and he just gave me a look somewhere between confusion and sympathy. Looking back, I think I now know why he then asked if and where I went to college. Emphasis on the *if*. Needless to say, I did not get that job. (My funniest work vocabulary fail is when I was in high school working at my after-school daycare job and heard the boss mention she might have to terminate one of the staff members. I was thinking, *Whoa, someone might get killed, I better shape up around here.*)

Once I made the decision to begin visiting restaurants, I made up some home-printed, amateur-looking business cards, put on my dad's tie, and grabbed a deck of playing cards and some coins. Then I drove from one restaurant to the next, walking in and asking for the GM. If they weren't there, I would ask when they would be there and come back at that time. If the GM *was* there, I introduced myself, asked if they were interested in hiring a magician, and offered to give a sample of the magic. As I faced rejection after rejection, it came to a point where I thought, *What if this doesn't work out? What will I do?* I remember pulling my car over at one point and praying for guidance and strength to keep going. Thankfully, the same possibility mindset I demonstrated at seven years old juggling the soccer ball was still alive inside me. I kept picking up the ball. I kept asking, *What else is possible?* As I mentioned earlier, over the course of a few weeks, I walked into forty restaurants and landed two. They were both Cajun restaurants, so I guess I had that "Louisiana" vibe about me. One of them was Copeland's of New Orleans, owned by former NFL player Neil Smith.

Forty restaurants. Thirty-eight rejections. I sound like a pretty patient person, huh? Well, when I tell people the stories of how I endured the restaurant-finding process, how I have persevered with soccer juggling, or how I've spent countless hours perfecting sleight of hand, people consistently tell me I must have an incredible amount of patience. But please hear me on this: All of my greatest accomplishments have had less to do with patience and more to do with passion. So many times, passion is mistaken for patience. If it was about mere patience I may have given up after walking into five restaurants. Think about the thing you love the most. Have you ever seemingly exhibited an unusual amount of patience when it comes to that one thing that you would say is typically above and beyond your normal threshold for patience? If you have, it's because your desire to master the skill, whether it's gaming or cooking or playing the violin, is stretching the boundaries of your patience. But you don't even notice. Your desire is urging you on and deepening your character. When it comes to that one thing, passion will create a level of "patience" you never dreamed you could have.

Well, the two restaurant jobs led to making connections, which led to performances in schools, churches, and living rooms, and before I knew it, a busy year had gone by. I took stock of the situation and realized I had made about the same amount of money as a first-year kindergarten teacher. That was all I needed to confirm I would not be going back for my master's degree. I didn't realize it at the time, but a little entrepreneurial fire had been lit inside me. In sticking with the theme of my vocabulary issues, I don't think I had ever even uttered the word entrepreneur up to that point. I had heard the word, but I just didn't really know what it meant. What I *did* know was that working for someone else was not going to be the best fit for me. I didn't know anything about business from a textbook standpoint or college classroom experience. I just knew nothing was going to stop me from achieving the seemingly impossible goal of becoming a professional magician. This was my calling. This was what I was going to do. Have you ever experienced the thrill of finding a way to make money doing something you love? Something where the hours just fly by as you do your work, impacting people and ending the day with a sense of satisfaction and fulfillment? If you have, you understand how exciting it was to make the decision to pursue magic as a vocation.

Even though I hadn't majored in business, I did have some innate business sense. I already had the magic part down, but quickly realized I needed to display an air of professionalism in order to close gigs and get spin-off bookings from my performances. That included the basics of dressing the part, paying close attention to my calendar, and showing up on time. It didn't take long to go from moderately dutiful college student to majorly responsible business owner. I had made commitments. People expected me to deliver. At a ripe twenty-four years old I was very quickly learning that dependability was not optional. I was recording every booking in my old-school planner, making note of how much I was charging for each performance, and checking it off when I got paid. Props to my dad for educating me about the need to pay taxes and pointing me to his tax service after the first year. Thankfully, even after taxes and expenses I was making a profit.

The Transition to Mentalism

With the first year of successful entrepreneurship under my belt, I would find my craft evolving considerably over the next nine years. Before I ever added motivational speaking, one major shift I made entertainment-wise was transitioning from magic to mentalism. What's the difference? In a nutshell, while magic is more visual in nature, mentalism is more psychological. Mentalism is a special flavor of magic, utilizing many of the same tactics used in magic to pull off illusions. It is seemingly doing things with your mind that science cannot explain. *Seemingly impossible* things. See why I love it?

The first time I watched someone perform mentalism, it was unlike anything I'd ever seen. What the entertainer was doing was not anything I was necessarily unfamiliar with, but how the crowd was responding was next level. I understood the mechanics behind his tricks, but jaws were hitting the floor, and people were out of their seats, totally amazed and bewildered. I knew I could master the tricks, but wondered if I could bring the showmanship and delivery style to create that type of response. Was it possible for me to perform like that? The answer was a *big yes*, of course, because something greater is always possible.

My magic-based show featured a cut-and-restored rope trick, the surprise appearance of an eight-foot wooden pole from a small brown paper bag, and the dramatic transformation of a floating origami rose into a real one—with a bright flash of fire (yes, it's as cool as it sounds!). Even though these tricks were amazing, I knew that mentalism was my destiny, to be dramatic. Once I discovered the impact of mentalism, I poured myself into the elevated presentation and delivery style, implementing new tricks like telling audience members what objects they were holding while I was blindfolded. One routine ends with me having predicted the serial number of an audience member's currency (that's a long series of numbers if you think about it). In another, I have two members from the audience on stage with their eyes closed. I tap one person on the shoulder and the person next to him feels it. It's really creepy—in a good way. The Envelope of Mystery and Vision Word tricks I use in my keynote fall into the category of mentalism.

All this isn't to say mentalism is superior to magic—it was just a better fit for my demeanor. The feedback from audience members was on a whole new level. As a result, I saw a higher demand for my services, so I ran with it. I cannot say enough for how embracing this nuance of magic called mentalism supercharged my career.

Explosive Business Growth

As my craft was evolving, so was my business. I kept adding tools and hacks and even today I'm constantly asking *what else is possible* for my business. Speaker and magician conferences were a great source of information about professional development, communication, and generating leads. At one conference in 2007, legendary comedy magician Michael Finney sat down with me one-on-one for over an hour to offer me some marketing tips that were *crucial* in enhancing my career.

Technology was also changing rapidly (when is it ever not?). Early on, I didn't even have a computer at home but would go to the library to check my email. (I wasn't excited about email, by the way: *Just call me on the phone, please!*) One day, my friend Roman said, "You should get devinhenderson.com." I agreed to let him build the site, even though I wasn't necessarily fired up about it and didn't care much about the content. But when he sent me the initial concept for the home page, something clicked. For the first time, I saw the potential—and I got excited about what this could mean for my career.

Once I realized the internet was here to stay, I began to take my online presence more seriously. I finally gave in and bought a computer to save me trips to the library. I started familiarizing myself with terms like SEO and meta tags. I was doing about everything I knew to do to get my name out there and get noticed by people who could hire me. Over time, as I handed out business cards and generated word-of-mouth referrals, small private parties eventually turned into corporate shows and magic/mentalism performances evolved into motivational keynotes. I slowly added elements of soccer, mentalism, and humor to my presentations, always asking what else was possible. That question, in one form or other, appears all throughout my magical journey.

These were all significant moments of growth for me, points of inspiration where I recognized what I wanted and began seeking it out. I realized when you're born to perform, you shouldn't and practically *can't* give up that dream. If you really believe something greater is always possible, you're always looking forward to the next thing, you're always seeking, because the solutions are there if the passion is strong enough. And as you continue to excel in all you do, key people are bound to take notice—eventually.

What else is possible?

CHAPTER FIVE

An Invitation from America's Got Talent

A PIVOTAL MOMENT IN my career came in 2014. At that time, I had been performing professionally for ten years, traveling all over the United States, blessed with the opportunity to entertain incredible groups of people. For a few years up to that time, I had also been producing YouTube videos featuring my magic because deep down, I wanted to reach more people. And even though things were going well, I couldn't help but wonder—when would I get my big break?

And then one day, totally out of the blue, I got *the* email—from *America's Got Talent*. It seemed too good to be true. At first, I wondered if the email was some weird spam or a joke from a friend, but it was legit. The email came from Carl, one of the casting agents from AGT. He said they were looking for a fresh act for season nine, that they had seen some of my videos on YouTube, and that I was exactly what they were looking for. This was the ultimate compliment because every piece of magic I do, especially the ones I put online, represents years of hard work and dedication.

Carl had invited me to audition for *America's Got Talent*—one of the biggest stages in the world. But this wasn't just any audition; I was heading straight to the celebrity stage in Hollywood, and I was honored by this personal invitation. It felt like all of my years of perseverance and hard work had finally paid off. It felt like a "chaos to order" kind of moment. And while I was super excited, there was a part of me that was afraid to fail. But then I thought—*What else is possible? What if this changes my life?* And you know what happened next? I said yes.

Before I tell the rest of the story, I want to share something with you that I share with my audiences. It's the best way I know of drawing people into the emotional impact this had on me at the time. For that, of course, I use a magic trick.

I hesitated including this trick here in the book, only because it's such a strong illusion that you have to see it to believe it. Then I decided to follow a wise piece of advice I once heard: "Just do it." Thanks, Nike.

I hold up a large white envelope with the *America's Got Talent* logo, signifying one of the email messages AGT sent me. I say "After I told them I was accepting their invitation, they sent me a message I'll never forget. I'll tell you what it is in just a minute." I then set the envelope aside.

"To help you understand how clarity came to me at that moment, let's demonstrate how things can magically come together."

I then ask the entire crowd to get out their cell phones. So go ahead, grab your phone. "Everyone bring up your calculators." You too. I then choose someone at random. "Can I please borrow your phone?"

I hop off the stage, take the person's phone and then hop back up on stage.

"We're going to do an equation using random audience members. If the Nerf ball comes to you, you'll call out any three-digit number."

I throw the ball into the audience. I say to the person who catches it, "Name a three-digit number."

Here, I will use the numbers that were chosen in my most recent keynote. The person said, "189."

As I put the digits 189 into the borrowed phone I say, "Everyone put 189 into your calculators then hit the multiplication button." You do it too. Then I say,

"Throw the ball." The ball is thrown and caught. "Name another three-digit number."

"387."

"Everyone put in the digits 387 and hit the multiplication button again." I do it along with them on the phone I borrowed, and you go ahead as well.

"Throw the ball one last time." The ball is thrown and caught. "Name a three-digit number."

"867."

"Everyone punch in 867." Go ahead and do it.

"Now we're going to mix it up. Everyone hit the subtraction button."

Now remember, I've been putting the equation into the borrowed phone. I then have the owner of the phone punch in several random digits into their phone, just wildly hitting buttons. When they're done, I say to the person, "I'm going to read off the number you punched in—make sure what I say is actually the number on your screen. Here it is—everyone subtract this number: 59152967. Now hit equals."

Just to make sure you've been following along, the equation was $189 \times 387 \times 867 - 59152967$. If you haven't already, hit the equals button.

"Someone read the answer."

Someone near the stage calls out, "4,262,014."

I say, "Is that the answer everyone got?" I hear many yeses. Is that what *you* got?

I then confirm that our answer is indeed 4,262,014, a seemingly random number. A number that was the result of a "chaotic process."

I continue, "That's how I felt with the grind and course of my career. I thought, 'What does all this mean? Where is this all going to ultimately land?' But remember, we're talking about chaos to order. Is there some kind of significance in what we just did? Let's find out." I then grab the *America's Got Talent* envelope and as I open it up, I continue talking,

"I'm a big believer in the idea that everything happens for a reason. After I told AGT 'I'm in,' they sent back a message. A message I told you I would never forget. It was the date for my audition." I pull out a folded-up paper banner from the envelope.

"That date just happened to be April 26th, 2014, or 4.26.2014." I spread my arms apart to reveal the five-foot-long banner with giant numbers that read "4.26.2014." That's when the audience realizes those digits perfectly match the digits on their phones— as it should on yours. It's a moment that begins with silence, followed by a crescendo of murmurs and gasps, then climaxes in a wild round of applause. I then let the banner fall to the ground in mic-drop fashion.

Just a quick aside here to reiterate the factors that make this illusion incredible: the audience members are all truly chosen at random. The equation is different in every performance. The answer is 4,262,014 for every, single, performance. Wait, what!? How is that possible? Mind-blowing, right? Man, I love what I do!

I continue, "So, chaos came to order. And by the way, *that's* the kind of trick that had AGT sending me straight to Hollywood."

Hollywood or Bust

About six months after the invite, AGT flew me to Hollywood and put me up in The Loews, a luxury hotel, all expenses paid. After I checked in, I walked down to the Dolby Theater, where they were filming auditions. I hung around backstage at the Dolby for about eight hours just waiting for the contestant interview that never happened. When they say showbiz is hard work, it's true! I was exhausted. But the next day, when it was time for the big audition in front of the celebrity panel, the adrenaline kicked in as I made my way back down to the theater. We finally did my on-camera interview, and then it was time to prepare for the performance.

I'll never forget those anxious moments just before my audition. When performing in large venues, I always try to get a glimpse of the crowd to prepare myself for what I'm walking into. I was able to peek out at the crowd. The Dolby Theater seats 3,300 people, my biggest audience up to that time. Not to mention, these 3,300 people were sitting right behind Howard Stern, Heidi Klum, Mel B, and Howie Mandel. *Nothing to be nervous about. I do this all the time. Just do what you do.* The next thing I knew, Nick Cannon, the host at the time, called me over to the entrance of the stage. With the camera in our faces, he said, "So Devin, what does *America's Got Talent* mean for you?"

I answered, "I guess it's just the next thing." Profound, I know.

Then Nick asked, "Are you ready?"

I said, "I was born ready."

He said, "Okay, you're on."

I was thinking, *Oh—right now?* I walked out onto that huge stage, and I still can't fully describe the moment. The blinding lights, the cameras, the celebrity judges, the massive crowd—it was totally surreal.

When I took center stage, Howard Stern said, "What's your name?"

"Devin." Should I have said my last name?

Then he said, "What do you do?"

"I do magic."

"All right, let's see what you got." Maybe you can hear his voice in your head.

Now, a couple of things made my performance special.

First, from what the producers told me, my act was the very first in the history of *America's Got Talent* in which they allowed on stage audience participation. I was the first one ever—pretty cool.

Second, I did one of my most difficult magic tricks, one that has a lot of unpredictable elements to it, but if everything goes right, it has a really high payoff. And you know what? I nailed it. I was very happy with my performance.

The third thing that made it special was the crowd. With that many people, it was a level of volume and energy I had never experienced before. They were engaged, we were laughing together, and at the end, they erupted in applause. It was hands down, to that day, the highest moment of my entire career.

At the conclusion of the trick, I told my volunteers they could have a seat. At that moment, I was elated. I did it. I succeeded. All of the reps over the years were finally going to pay off in a very big way. Just from this one appearance, regardless of how far I went beyond that point, my popularity was going to shoot through the roof, my social media following was sure to blow up, and ah, the endless selfie requests to come from strangers everywhere I went.

And then I heard the sound that changed everything.

Buzzzzzzzzzzzzzz!!!

Wait—did I really just get buzzed? I looked behind me and saw one of the red *X*'s lit up. *What? That must have been an accident, because I just crushed it.* They had warned us backstage that if we got buzzed, get ready, it is very loud. Very. Loud. They weren't lying. Mel B had buzzed me. A very profound silence descended on the auditorium.

Howard said, "Mel B, you exed him. You go first."

Mel B said, "What was that? You said you're a magician. I was expecting some magical thing. I like your look, I like your style, but I thought it would end with something spectacular. I could probably do what you just did." Really? Okay.

Then back to Howard: "That's a great trick. I wish I could do that trick. I'm just not sure that it plays to this big of an audience."

Then it was Howie's turn: "I have friends who do a very similar routine," I held my breath as the possibility of an ally surfaced, "but they do it *really* well." Meaning better. I get it. Then he went on to tell me ways I could improve the trick, and the audience, who sixty seconds earlier loved me, turned on me and started to agree with him by applauding his remarks. Mob mentality is great only when the mob loves you.

Heidi offered a bright spot in an otherwise tough moment. She leaned into the mic and told me she disagreed with the others— she loved the act—and she was a solid "yes." It wasn't enough to move me forward, but it gave me something positive to hold on to. Unfortunately, with only one vote in my favor, I was still two short of success. Then came Howard's response. He looked straight at me and delivered the words I was hoping not to hear: "Sorry, but it's just not what we're looking for." And just like that, it was over.

The Audition's Impact

The next few minutes were kind of a blur—producers offering awkward "it's okay"s while I made my way backstage, took off the microphone, and started feeling that slow pull toward acceptance. With a heavy heart, I retraced the steps to the upscale hotel room. The beautiful day I had experienced on the walk to the theater seemed like a dream, or nightmare, as the shock of what had just happened started to sink in. There goes the big social media following and selfies. I was devastated. As I made my way down the crowded sidewalk with my tail between my legs, I considered the possibility of quitting magic. The thing I had been doing since I was eleven years old. The thing I loved. The thing I knew I was good at. The thing that supported my family. I wanted to take all the props and my magic tricks I had invested hours and hours in and throw them all into the ocean. I wanted to be done with magic forever.

Have you ever been there? Have you ever felt you delivered your very best only to get the opposite response you expected? Have you ever invested countless hours, or maybe even years, into something only to experience massive disappointment?

Have you ever just wanted to *quit*?

Fortunately, I had only told a handful of people about the AGT audition, so I wouldn't need to explain the result to too many people. While I was still in Hollywood, my booking coordinator, Crystal, kept sending texts asking how things were going. I put off replying and telling her what happened, but I eventually did. What was depressing was that I was by myself. Alone in "La La Land" with no one to encourage me or just sit and be sad with me. What made it even worse was knowing Lynn and the girls, my best unconditional comforters, were half the country away. There was nothing I wanted to do more than hop on a plane and get out of there, but unfortunately my flight wasn't until the next day.

So I ended up walking up and down Hollywood Boulevard, spinning tales of *what if* in my head. What if I hadn't been such a rule-follower and had gone over my time limit of ninety seconds? It turns out lots of people did that. I felt so rushed. What if I had kindly asked for a chance to come back at another time and show them the kind of magic that would blow them away? What if I had requested to do another trick in the moment? I've seen people defend themselves and make it through. What if I had tried a little harder to stay alive?

Then the excuses started. I was sleep deprived. I was under tremendous pressure. It was their idea for me to do that specific trick in the first place. Shouldn't the producers, of all people, guide me in the right direction? It was too overwhelmingly stressful to have the presence of mind to make the best choices in those moments. Maybe the volunteers I chose were not outgoing enough. Maybe my hair didn't look good. Maybe my jacket was wrinkled.

The truth was I had done my best and things hadn't worked out the way I hoped they would. Pretty simple, but it was hard to turn off the narrative playing in my head.

I finally made it home to my wife and kids, hoping I could shake it off and get back to real life. I did everything I could think of to find a silver lining to the situation. For instance—even before the AGT audition, I had started to lose interest in magic and had been considering switching exclusively to comedy or motivational speaking to change things up. If I had made it through, it might have pigeonholed me strictly into magic for the rest of my life, so maybe it was a good thing I didn't succeed. But those thoughts did nothing to help my emotions rebound from that epic failure.

Night after night, thoughts of missed opportunities kept me awake. It felt like I had missed something huge. I couldn't stop thinking about how my social media following could have sky-rocketed, how my success with AGT would have bought me more credibility to get bigger, higher-paying jobs. I could have been recognized in more places and been hired because I was the *America's Got Talent* guy. Then there was the possibility of that million dollars if I had won the entire competition. This could have been a game changer for my career, for my life, for everything.

To top it all off, the segment never aired on TV. They didn't even post it on YouTube. It was like it never happened. I'm still not sure if that was a good thing or a bad thing, but it did nothing for my self-esteem at the time.

For the next year or so, I struggled with deep sadness. I wouldn't go so far to say it was clinical depression, but it was a major shift in my emotions that I couldn't get a handle on. It felt too embarrassing to talk to anyone about what I had been through, so I just retreated within myself. I remember sitting at the breakfast table and feeling my mouth literally drooping in sadness. Like I couldn't keep the despair inside from becoming visible on the outside. One day my daughter looked at my wife and said, "What's wrong with Dad?" I just didn't want to go on with magic. I didn't feel like doing any of my work tasks. All I could do was imagine what could have been, the missed potential, the fractured seemingly impossible goal.

Have you ever been in a position where the typical positive thinking was doing nothing to help? You knew the right things to do and say, but you just couldn't find the energy to make it happen? I felt as though no one could relate to my emotions.

In those moments walking down Hollywood Boulevard and sitting around the breakfast table, I knew I needed the possibility mindset more than ever. So what if I'd been voted off *America's Got Talent*, missing a shot at fame and fortune? Deep down, I knew those things were never going to bring lasting joy anyway. But my pride and ego just wouldn't let go of those desires. I tried time and time again to imagine what else was possible, but I was in too much pain. I wanted to pick up the ball, a practice I was used to every day. I thrived on failure, or at least I mostly had up to this point, but the blow had been too severe. It was a deeper level of discouragement than I had ever experienced before in my professional career.

This kind of devastation paralyzed me in a completely unexpected way. I needed something else, another solution to pull me up and get me going again.

What else is possible?

CHAPTER SIX

A Whole New Meaning to AGT

WELL, SPOILER ALERT—I didn't quit performing magic. But I seriously considered it. And if I had given into those negative feelings, who knows what I'd be doing today? Would I be performing at all? Would I be speaking? Would you be reading these words right now?

It's possible to stay mentally and physically healthy, even in the midst of emotional distress—*as long as you stay aware of your emotions and actively manage them.* That's why it's so important to challenge the negative voices in your head. The journey to greatness is emotional by nature, which is exactly why I stress the power of positive emotions in the Envelope of Mystery illusion. Whether you're chasing success in your personal or professional life, emotions shape how you respond, decide, and keep moving forward.

So, I *didn't* quit, but how did I keep going? More importantly, how can *you* pursue *your* goals when you feel like you can't? How do you stop fearing the worst and start hoping for the best, even when things don't always turn out the way you expected? Keep reading.

On the Brink of Breakthrough

At first, my impulse was to hide what happened with my Hollywood experience because I felt embarrassed and ashamed. But it was when I finally decided to start talking about it openly to more people that I began to heal. The simple fact I had gotten through those hard days made it possible for me to inspire others. Especially once I brought it to my keynote stage and exposed my story publicly, the humbling experience began turning into a good thing. It was not only an interesting and entertaining story, but it resonated with audiences who could identify with big disappointments. It created a connection to help them see that failures, even really big ones, are oftentimes blessings in disguise. It finally became clear to me that remaining immobile and sad was not the best thing for me, for those around me, and for those I serve. I needed to refocus and somehow find the positivity in my life; the young Devin who never saw an obstacle he couldn't get over was still inside me somewhere.

But changing my thought patterns was easier said than done. Every time I heard the words *America's Got Talent* or AGT, it triggered me. My mind immediately returned to the giant buzzer and all that came after it. It caused me pain. I would lose a grasp on my emotions. Maybe you have a similar trigger word tied to pain or stress. It's a visceral reaction that can anger us, bring us to tears, or make us feel hopeless. If this is your experience, you're not alone. I get it. But I also know there comes a time when you can not only get back on your feet, but stand stronger than ever.

AGT Redefined

So what was my turning point?

It was in the summer of 2017, three years after my audition. I had come a long way in moving past those negative feelings, but they were still hanging on to a degree. Otherwise, at that point, life was good. Business was fine. My family was healthy, and overall things were going well. I was in Las Vegas to deliver a keynote and walking down the Strip, just enjoying the beautiful day. Suddenly, I came upon the LINQ Hotel, where Mat Franco's twenty-foot-tall image took up a good portion of the side of the building. In case you're not a devoted follower of *America's Got Talent*, I'm talking about Mat Franco, magician and winner of AGT season nine. Sound familiar *now*? We auditioned the same day. We hung out backstage and talked all things magic. He was actually a really great dude, by the way, and we had essentially been equals the day of our auditions. We performed just a few minutes apart, but I was kicked off immediately, and he went all the way—won the whole thing. A million bucks. Headlining in Vegas. That could've been *my* picture on that building. I was *so* close. Three years after the fact, all that pain hit me harder than it ever had. Boom. Right in the gut—like I had gotten the wind knocked out of me.

And then, out of nowhere, in the midst of my pain, reflection, and prayers, a new realization hit me, and it changed everything: *If things had not happened the way they had, we wouldn't have our youngest kid* (now four youngest kids, because we've had three since that insight). It's obvious when you think about it, but I'll explain. If things had gone differently in the past, they would have affected future outcomes. A number of things could possibly be different for Lynn and me right now—for example, where we live or, most notably and relevant here, our timing with conception. At the time of my AGT audition, we had just four children. If things hadn't turned out exactly the way they did, I can now say we wouldn't have our four youngest treasures—who mean more to me than winning any competition ever could.

On top of that, we wouldn't have the life we've built here in Kansas City—close to dear friends and family, raising our girls in a place that just feels like home. While the Las Vegas entertainment scene works well for a lot of people, I knew it wasn't where I was meant to be. It was almost like the future I didn't get flashed before my eyes, and all of a sudden it wasn't so appealing. I was so overcome with gratitude for the life I was living. And I realized in that moment that I wouldn't give up any of it for the money or my face on the side of a building or millions of social media followers.

That's when I saw it—something that completely transformed how I was feeling and that can transform you too. Something that deepened my renewed sense of gratitude and, to this day, continues to bring me peace and strength whenever I'm wrestling with unrest and regret. I saw it in the letters AGT, as in *America's Got Talent*. Despite, or perhaps because of, the pain associated with those words, they instantly took on a new meaning, and suddenly I could see new possibilities again. Now, AGT means this:

A lways
G ive
T hanks

Crazy simple. Insanely powerful. But not the easiest to apply in our hardest moments. However, when you resolve to shift your focus to deep gratitude and gain a new perspective, wonderful and magical things start to happen.

You begin to feel the relief of accepting what is, and you also open the door to forgiving yourself for any past mistakes. You start to focus on what's good. And—you begin experiencing another breakthrough within the possibility mindset.

Here are some powerful reflections during times of disappointment:

- What if there was some greater reason for this outcome?

WHEN YOU RESOLVE TO
SHIFT YOUR FOCUS
TO DEEP
GRATITUDE
AND GAIN A
NEW PERSPECTIVE,
WONDERFUL
AND MAGICAL THINGS
START TO
HAPPEN

- What's some way this seemingly negative situation might bless you today?
- What if something that felt like failure might bless you down the road?

Questions like these can help you take control of your emotions by changing the way you look at any predicament, no matter how disappointing. Even failure. *Especially* failure.

The *America's Got Talent* experience taught me that failure is not a dead end. Failure is just a fork in the road. That means you have the opportunity to choose the path of growth over the path of giving up. The path of endless possibility over the path of self-destruction. In other words, as I so charismatically state in my keynote because of the poet I am deep down:

> *You can choose to let failure*
> *Make you—not break you*
> *Hone you—not own you*
> *Carry you—not bury you*
> *But you do have to choose, to let failure*
> *Revitalize you—not paralyze you*
> *Bless you—not depress you*
> *Revive you—not deprive you*
> *And most importantly, you can let failure*
> *Refine you—not define you*
> *So, when hard things happen—may the forks be with you.*

It was time to shift focus once and for all from what could have been to what was. Time to move toward the future that the possibility mindset was opening up before me. Time to remove the power that colossal failure was still holding over my thoughts and emotions. Time to be thankful. Time to realize that greater things were still possible, because greater things are *always* possible.

New possibilities start with a change in perspective, and gratefulness will not only help you discover those opportunities but will also help you see the treasure that already exists in your life. It will help open your eyes to it. It's a tool that can elevate you when you feel all hope is lost.

And it can start right now. You can decide you're the kind of person who never stops being thankful. Oftentimes when we are in emotional pain about one thing, we tend to overlook the riches we already have. The things we cherish most. So, when the next tough moment hits, instead of asking the question, "Will I ever get through this?" try asking:

- What *else* do I have to be grateful for?
- What *is* working in my life?

There's *always* something.

Perhaps you are in a tough spot right now. The pain you're experiencing is overwhelming and seems to be all you can think about. I am not trying to downplay what you are going through; I simply want to encourage you to take the next step forward. Try adding just one new positive thought to your inner dialogue. Do you have a loving family? Give thanks for that huge blessing. Are you in good health? Celebrate that. Are you someone with solid character? Acknowledge the people who influenced you. Are you in good shape financially? Be grateful you don't have to worry about money. Is your team at work on fire? Recognize the impact you're making together. Always give thanks.

Modeling Gratitude, Eventually

Gratitude is essential for being a good parent. It helps me shift negative reactions in my mind before they turn into the kind of behavior frustration might provoke—like snapping, shutting down, or overreacting.

Several Christmases ago, I took my two oldest kids and a friend of theirs to pick out a tree. Being the suburban dad that I am, I took the kids to a big-box home store down the road instead of a classic Christmas tree farm. Honestly, I'd prefer the charm and nostalgia of a real tree farm—but for some reason, they're never open around here when I actually need them. We put on some Christmas tunes, the girls were laughing together, and it started out as a great adventure. We found a good tree, and as I was tying it to the top of the car, I noticed the kids had walked out with hot chocolates. This is a very sweet gesture on the store's part, but there was one problem—no lids. My mind immediately went to negativity: *Come on, big-box home store, ya gotta put lids on hot beverages before handing them to children.*

I gave the girls a warning to be careful and not spill their hot chocolates as they got in the car, because giving warnings is always an effective parenting technique. Uh-huh, *totally*. They acknowledged me with, "Yeah, okay, sure thing." Two seconds later I heard, "Whoops." I looked in the car and there was hot chocolate all over the back seat. Spills of any kind are one of my least favorite things—just ask my wife and kids. Plug yourself into this moment with me: holiday stress, three kids, and a huge mess. Does this change your attitude? Does it affect your behavior?

I was angry when I opened my door to get in and slammed it a little harder than usual in that awkward dad way. I started the car, and the happy Christmas music came on. I turned it off—no, I *shut* it off. That made it even easier to hear my daughters' friend say, "Your dad's mad."

My oldest said, "Yeah, he gets this way."

I could hear the record scratch in my head. *I get this way?* She was right, as she is about my attitude a lot of the time, and it got my attention. Here I was, a motivational speaker, and I couldn't even keep my own thoughts on a positive track over a little hot chocolate spill. It was time to harness a spirit of gratitude to save this sad situation. I began to count my blessings, starting with the most obvious: our good vehicle, no ice on the roads, and enjoying my favorite season of the year by heading to my warm home to decorate a tree with my healthy and beautiful wife and daughters. I was not going to let a spill rob my kids and me of this memory, and now that gratitude was in play, I decided that all we needed next was a touch of humor to turn this thing completely around.

I looked up in the rearview mirror and in good dad-joke fashion asked, "I have to know, girls—who peed hot chocolate all over the seat?" All of a sudden we were laughing, I turned the music back on, and the Christmas spirit returned. Gratefulness combined with a little humor saved the day.

It's important to model this principle for my children, as life will not always go their way. It's important to teach them that, no matter how bad things may seem, something good is always happening. Study after study affirms that those who practice gratitude experience better health, stronger relationships, and greater life satisfaction. The emotional and spiritual benefits manifest themselves in physical ways. There is simply no downside to being thankful.

My friend Cam writes in a gratitude journal first thing every morning. Before looking at his phone or checking his email when he wakes up, before doing anything, Cam writes down ten things he's grateful for. The catch here is they need to be ten things he hasn't already written, so by the end of the year he has thousands of concrete words of gratefulness to reflect on. Cam is actively resetting his thought patterns each day to put him on a positive path. How can a practice like that not impact a person in a powerful way?

Gratitude absolutely has the power to shift our perspective—but here's something else to consider: Maybe our greatest battles aren't with circumstances. Maybe they're with the illusions we've created in our own minds. What if the thing holding you back isn't even real?

What else is possible?

CHAPTER SEVEN

Pause, Pivot, Pull

HAVE YOU EVER doubted your worth in your work despite your experience, talent, or passion? Or do you ever feel stuck about what to do next because there are too many tasks or choices in front of you? You may have your own special blend of mental obstacles that threaten your success. Regardless of your profession or various roles in your personal life, these unproductive thoughts can sneak in at any time, sabotaging your possibilities. This can cause you to see lies about yourself and your situation and accept those lies as truth. Believing lies can make you feel like your hands are tied, so to speak, preventing your freedom to move forward. Even if you are a strong and resilient person, sometimes this struggle can hold you back from realizing your potential.

These lies are, of course, not reality but illusion. And when we become hyperfocused on the *proverbial ropes* binding our wrists, the hold can feel tighter and tighter. We end up exhausting ourselves fighting a phantom force, wearing ourselves out in a struggle against something that was never truly there. So how do we break free of the lies that threaten to block our progress? How can we escape this trap and pursue greater possibilities again? By separating reality from illusion.

And who better to help separate reality from illusion than an *illusionist*? In my keynote, I use a magic trick to illustrate this concept. I choose two volunteers to tie my wrists very tightly together with a piece of rope. It's kind of like Houdini—just without being tossed into a river. Then, I have the volunteers hold up a large black cloth in front of me, big enough to hide my hands from the audience.

As I explain that I'm about to attempt a record-breaking escape and how difficult this trick is, I occasionally raise one hand above the cloth—completely free of the rope—to give subtle directions like, "Take a step back" or "Hold the cloth a little higher." It's all part of the act. The free hand is a deliberate distraction, used to manipulate the volunteers without ever acknowledging that it's not actually tied. Then I drop that hand back behind the cloth, and when both hands rise again—this time clearly bound—I carry on as if nothing unusual just happened.

It takes the crowd a few seconds to realize what's going on, and they start to laugh. They know one hand was free, they just don't know how. It usually takes the volunteers on stage longer to recognize what's at play since I'm keeping their attention on their tasks, but typically they catch on too and join in the laughter. After comedically "escaping" a few times, I finally toss the rope to the stage and shake hands with the volunteers.

You know how I told you I wouldn't reveal any secrets of magic? Well, I'll make an exception here, since I also share this with the audience because it's the perfect way to illustrate a powerful concept. Besides, you've come with me this far, so you've earned it. Are you ready for the secret? Here it is:

Pause. Pivot. Pull.

Okaaaay—what in the world does that mean? I'll explain.

When the volunteers tie the knots in the rope, the rope is undetectably crisscrossed so that it appears to be tightly wound around both wrists. Just after they tie my wrists, I show the audience how tight the ropes are by "struggling" to get free. With the ropes still crossed, they truly are tight and I very much look like and feel trapped, kind of like how we can feel *mentally* trapped at times. But once I *pause* from the struggle, and simply *pivot* my hands, the rope uncrosses and therefore loosens just enough to allow me to *pull* my hands free. Then I'm able to escape the illusion almost instantly and also reverse the process and stick my hands back in at the same speed for comedic effect.

Pause, Pivot, Pull: That's the process for breaking free when illusions threaten to hold you back from greatness. Many times when you're struggling to get free from an obstacle, it's possible you're fighting nothing more than an illusion. Breaking free is simply a matter of Pause, Pivot, Pull.

Let's look at three typical "illusions" in which you break free by applying this process.

The Illusion of Insignificance

The Illusion of Insignificance says that because someone is farther along than you, then what you're doing is meaningless. This illusion is something that can seem so real, it can make you feel worthless, inferior, and really choke your creativity. Have you ever experienced these feelings because you negatively compared yourself to someone else? I haven't.

Just kidding, I have.

At one point in my soccer juggling journey, when I was about nineteen years old, my record was around 2,000 kicks. Then my priorities shifted with college, and then marriage and parenting, and soccer went on the back burner. When I picked it up again, I looked on YouTube to see what other people had accomplished. I found one person who had done 4,000 kicks—double my record at the time. This person just so happened to be a girl named Mya who was only eight years old. That bothered me—not because she was a girl (girls are awesome—they're all my wife and I make, remember?) but because she was so young. I thought, *If someone less than half my age has accomplished double the kicks I have, what's the point? Should I just give up now?* Then I thought, *Well, if she can do it, it is possible.* And since I wanted to keep progressing with my soccer kicks anyway, I thought, *Challenge accepted, kiddo.* I decided to not believe the lie that her success somehow meant I couldn't succeed, and instead of letting it stop me, I let it fuel me. And that accelerated me on the path to get to where I am today.

Do you ever compare yourself negatively to the people around you? Maybe even your teammates? This can really disrupt an effective working relationship. It's not healthy for you or for anyone around you. The fear of being shown up by your coworkers can drive you toward unhealthy autonomy and isolation, but effective teamwork requires that we lean on our teammates and strive to work together. Like Helen Keller said, "Alone we can do so little; together we can do so much."

What if comparison didn't have to hold you back?

Refusing to believe the Illusion of Insignificance is a simple idea, but not necessarily easy. In fact, it's something I have to be mindful of even now, and I'll tell you what I mean.

Sometimes when I tell people I achieved over 11,000 kicks, a number I'm proud of, they ask me if I'm in the *Guinness Book of World Records*. I joke and say, "Yeah, I'm in it. I read it all the time," because I'm totally hilarious. But no, my name is not in the book. And while I joke about it, that can discourage me and make me think, *What's the point? Sure, I've kicked the ball for two continuous hours, but the Guinness World Record is kicking for thirty hours.*

(Based on my research, Guinness apparently allows a five-minute break each hour. Still super impressive, but what's up with that?)

The reality is that no matter what you've achieved or how impressive your accomplishments are, there will almost always be someone better than you, further along than you, doing things you wish you were doing. But you have the opportunity to decide how to respond to that knowledge. Do you let discouragement and doubt overwhelm you, or do you use the energy of someone else's greatness to propel you forward?

When you find yourself feeling insignificant because you're stuck in the comparison trap, how do you break free?

That brings us back to Pause, Pivot, Pull.

As you read this next part, physically do what I ask of my audiences. Are you ready? Okay, put your wrists together as if they're tied, like in my trick. You should look like you're in a praying position. But imagine as if you don't realize it's an illusion. You truly feel trapped. You're struggling, feeling insignificant and frustrated with the fact that someone else is further along than you. Now:

- **PAUSE**. Stop struggling. Catch yourself saying and believing the lie, "That person is better than me."
- **PIVOT**. This is accomplished by flipping the lie into a truth, like this: "That person is better than me—at being who *they* are." As you say this, keep your wrists touching, but rotate your hands so that your fingers are now pointing in opposite directions. This is the secret to loosening the ropes.
- **PULL**. Then you can *pull* free and recognize that other people's greatness does not threaten your greatness. Now, pull your hands apart and feel the freedom that comes with this process.

Doesn't that feel awesome, knowing that your greatness doesn't have to be overshadowed by others? Along with that—what if your goal wasn't to be *the* best, but to be *your* best . . . and what if your best *is* the best to the people you are meant to serve?

Because if you aren't using your greatness in service to others, *what is the point?* If greatness is about you—it will never be good enough. But if it's about serving others, you can rise above The Illusion of Insignificance.

The Illusion of Can't

The Illusion of Can't says that because you can't do it *now*, you can't do it *ever*.

Parents of small children tend to hear "I can't" on a regular basis. I know I do. "I can't get this lid off." "I can't zip up my jacket." "I can't find my other shoe."

When this happens, I tell my kids, "Stop saying I can't."

They say, "I can't."

From these words, spoken out of frustration or at times exhaustion, I have found that these precious ones can learn the positive language of "I can" when I'm patient enough to take the time to help them see they have abilities beyond what they currently believe. "Yes, you *can* zip up your jacket, if you do it like this. And the more you work at it, the better you'll get." But it's not only kids who deal with the Illusion of Can't.

In my work I use my hands. In fact, it seems most of the hobbies and activities I've been a part of involve my hands (even with my soccer juggling, like when I spin the ball on my finger). In every hands-on activity, from piano to drums to guitar to magic, I never expected to accomplish any of it immediately.

During college, there were a few people who asked me to teach them some chords on the guitar. Like most skills, it's easier than it looks. When people would try to first form a chord, I remember a common response being something along the lines of, "I can't do it. My fingers won't do that." The same thing happens when people see me cut a deck of cards with one hand, called the one-handed cut or the Charlier Cut. When people ask if I'll show them how to do it, I'm happy to. I demonstrate it slowly for them, and as they're trying it, I coach them along. I typically get the same response as with the guitar chords: "I can't. My hand just won't do that. My fingers aren't long enough. My hands aren't big enough. I'm not built for this. I can't do it."

Have you ever reacted like this when trying something new? Just remember—your ultimate success isn't about being able to do everything immediately. It's about learning. It's about showing up and trying. Even when you commit to starting ugly and starting small, there's an illusion looming in the shadows, waiting to trip you up. It's the Illusion of Can't—and if you start believing the story that you can't, it can start to feel real. Real enough to make picking up the ball seem pointless.

So how do you escape this illusion? Once again, you Pause, Pivot, Pull. (Remember to go through the physical motions as you read this to help you not just visualize but actually experience the breaking-free process. So go ahead and get those wrists back together.)

- **PAUSE.** Stop struggling. Catch yourself saying and believing the lie, "I can't."
- **PIVOT.** How could you flip what you're saying so it is true? "I can't . . . yet, but one day I will."
- **PULL.** And now that you see the truth, you can *pull* free of the illusion and move forward.

What does that look like for your life? Maybe the thing tying you down is specific, like "I can't close this sale" or "I can't help this patient" or "I can't learn this system." Maybe your bondage is a broader problem, like "I can't lead these people" or "I can't help transform this culture" or "I can't find reliable employees." These situations may seem hopeless, but if you Pause, Pivot, and Pull against the Illusion of Can't, you can escape those mental traps with ease. Flip those lies into truth, and the truth will set you free.

I had my own recent experience with the Illusion of Can't, which came up when I was thinking about writing this very book. Will Severns, cofounder of Streamline (my publisher), was exactly who I needed to help me Pause, Pivot, and Pull my way out of feeling like I could never do it. This is how that process unfolded:

- **PAUSE**. I caught myself saying, "I'll never have the capacity to write a book."
- **PIVOT**. Then I flipped it into something true: "I'll never have the capacity to write a book . . . unless I find qualified people to help me get it done."
- **PULL**. I finally decided to *pull* the trigger and am literally writing the book right now.

That's an especially exciting one for me. I had an important goal but felt like my hands were tied because of a lack of time and publishing expertise. It may have taken years for me to figure out how to do this on my own. Streamline provided professional project management, editing, artwork, and publishing services. Now you are holding the results of this unbeatable strategy in your hands.

Another example of Pause, Pivot, Pull came from a moment on my podcast, *The Possibility Mindset*. My good friend and mentor Mark Mayfield, who is a Hall of Fame Speaker and author of the foreword of this book, shared some key insights into heavy topics like stress, anxiety, and self-harm. He described the practice of *pausing* when you encounter stress, then engaging in *pivotal* activities you enjoy, such as listening to music or calling a friend. This, he says, is one effective way of *pulling* out of the funk when you feel anxious or depressed.

Clifton Alexander was another guest on my podcast who brought some Pause, Pivot, Pull wisdom of his own. Clifton is a longtime friend and award-winning founder of Kansas City-based REACTOR Design. He taught me this jewel when you want something that feels out of reach because you're at someone else's mercy: *Just ask*. It's simple, yet brilliant: Pause and then pivot by asking for what you want. "If there's something in front of you and there's a person who's essentially the gatekeeper to that thing, just ask. If you don't ask, you're not going to know," he shared.

Clifton says this strategy has been working for him ever since he was an art student needing to gain access to a restricted area for a photo shoot. He simply approached the gatekeeper, in this case the security guard who literally held the keys, and just asked. The next thing Clifton knew, he was climbing stairs to the perfect vantage point for his photos. Today, he models the *just ask* idea at work and with his family, even in low-risk settings such as restaurants: "I might go in with my family and be seated where we don't want to be. I'll just ask, 'Can we sit over there?' The worst thing that happens is they say no, but at least we tried."

You can apply these winning principles to your thought processes moving forward. Maybe you can even commit to reevaluating goals from the past that you would still love to achieve. Is there a personal or professional dream that once held a prominent place in your mind but has become more unfocused as time has passed? Reject the Illusion of Can't and claim that dream once again. Commit to yourself and to the people around you to complete the words "I can't" with the word "... yet." That phrase is contagious, and so is the attitude that comes with it. Remember that "can" is a process, and as a result, you won't buy into the Illusion of Can't.

The Illusion of Impossible

The Illusion of Impossible is more than just thinking "I can't." It's when your mind uses anything negative about you, no matter how mean, to make you feel hopeless. To make you want to quit. Let me give you an example.

My soccer and magic demonstrations on stage are just a highlight reel. The audience is not seeing the behind-the-scenes moments when picking up the ball was hard. During my soccer training, every so often I would yell out of frustration or feel the urge to kick the ball through a window. Sometimes, after struggling to master more difficult moves, I would resolve never to kick the ball again. This would happen when I temporarily bought into the illusion that reaching my goal wasn't possible. And then my own mind would hurl insults, with no jab being off the table.

That critical side of me would say, *You idiot. You're just wasting your time. You should have been able to do this by now because you've been working on it for so long.* It didn't take long for that voice to make me feel hopeless and nearly resolve to quit.

Have you ever heard that voice?

It becomes strongest when we temporarily buy into the Illusion of Impossible.

If you believe this illusion is real, you may just quit. But you can also see these moments as indicators that you're on the right track, pursuing something significant. These feelings are to be expected when you're working toward any important goal over a period of time.

So how do you snap out of it when the Illusion of Impossible feels overwhelming and real? How do you move past the temptation to give up? Well, Pause, Pivot, Pull has a little different flavor when it comes to this illusion, but the same basic structure applies.

- **PAUSE.** When you feel compelled to quit, go ahead and let yourself say the words, "I give up." (Talk about a serious pause.)
- **PIVOT.** How could you flip what you're saying into something that will in turn help you keep going? "I give up . . . temporarily."
- **PULL.** Once you allow yourself a much-needed break, you can *pull* yourself back into action.

(Did you remember to do the hand motions that time? They serve as a powerful memory tool, and I hope those movements become second nature any time you're struggling.)

Sometimes, giving up temporarily just means stepping away. That could look like walking around the block, taking a day or two off, or securing a longer break if needed. In some cases, stepping away might lead to deeper reflection and bigger shifts—like reworking your entire approach, moving to a new city, or reevaluating a relationship. The point isn't to quit forever. It's to step back long enough to gain perspective, restore your energy, and return with renewed purpose—even if the path forward ends up looking a little different.

In my soccer juggling journey, there have been times when I've let myself put the soccer ball down for weeks and sometimes months. And guess what? I came back refreshed and even more energized to succeed. As busy parents, sometimes my wife and I need a break. Our brains are on overload, and we feel like it's nearly impossible to help settle another LEGO dispute, or help the kids decide on a movie that will make *everyone* happy, or ya know—other first-world problems. Weekly date nights and regular getaways have been powerful ways for us to reconnect and recharge—allowing us to love, lead, and serve our children with even greater strength and presence.

Many times, all you need is a little break to break through the Illusion of Impossible.

My "Boulder" Pause

Depending on the circumstance, choosing to pause and step away can be a painful process for both you and others. Oftentimes, though, it can be the key to moving forward with peace and confidence.

One major pause in my life was the extended break Lynn and I took from dating. Remember how I told you earlier that marriage was something I had a hard time envisioning? Even after meeting this beautiful, amazing woman, my worries about such a tremendous commitment not only remained a struggle—they intensified. Lynn and I had been a couple for about a year and a half, and everything seemed just right. We had a great time together, our spiritual beliefs and values aligned, we both loved and wanted kids, and everything looked perfect from the outside. Everyone assumed it was just a matter of time before we got engaged.

However, finding complete clarity felt nearly impossible—doubt still clung to me. Was Lynn truly the one? Were we moving too fast? Were we being swept along by others' expectations instead of following our own instincts?

In the midst of this uncertainty, Lynn offered a powerful metaphor: a massive rock blocking our path—we called it *the boulder*. Looking back, she described how, as we moved toward this looming obstacle—really a reflection of my internal struggle—she began to feel pieces of it breaking off and hitting her. But at the time, she couldn't see the boulder. It was still too far off, hidden from view. The fragments—my moments of doubt, my comments about needing space—seemed to come out of nowhere. It wasn't until the boulder finally came into sight that everything clicked. The source of those fragments was suddenly clear. And in hindsight, all of it had foreshadowed the pause that was coming.

Eventually, we reached the boulder. I needed to explore the depths of my heart and mind, so we took separate paths—me going one way around it, Lynn the other. The boulder was too big to see beyond. Would our paths reconnect on the other side? Or had we already begun to part for good?

The trek around the boulder lasted five months. I kept wondering if there really was one person out there meant for me—or if that was just a romantic fairy tale I'd always told myself. I took many walks in nature and wrestled with the thought of marriage rather than just jumping in because it was the next step in a process. I think a lot of people refuse to take time for introspection before marriage, and that can end up being a big mistake because they look back and think, "Dang, I should have paused." For me, this pause was crucial—marriage was a serious commitment, because according to everything I believe in, saying "I do" meant a lifetime.

The emotions I was wrestling with had nothing to do with whether Lynn was good enough—she was extraordinary. What I was really confronting was myself, and the weight of what "us" truly meant. There was no going back to just being boyfriend and girlfriend. The path ahead was clear: Either we part ways for good, or I ask her to be my wife. Many people didn't understand that I needed time and space to process it all in my own way. I get it—on the outside, I probably looked heartless. But one thing I've learned is this: I have to be okay with being misunderstood. I can't please everyone, and as long as I'm anchored in integrity and guided by honor, I don't need to chase approval.

Am I suggesting everyone take a five-month break from their significant other before getting married? No. I'm simply sharing my experience to illustrate that some of life's biggest decisions may benefit from intentional pause and consideration.

Thankfully, Lynn was incredibly patient, loving, and understanding. She knew me well—and she knew that what I was wrestling with carried lifelong implications for us both. After those five months, I felt reassured that our paths were meant to meet again—just on the other side of the boulder. In that *pause*, stillness, reflection, and prayer became *pivotal* practices that helped me break free from fear and doubt, guiding me to a place of clarity, confidence, and peace.

When I shared this with Lynn, it gave her peace too. And thankfully, when I *pulled* out the ring, she said yes.

What else is possible?

CHAPTER EIGHT

What's Your Magic?

ONCE YOU'VE BROKEN free of any restraining illusions using Pause, Pivot, Pull, it's time to ask *what else is possible* in terms of the freedom you can experience that will enable you to fully live out your purpose. What could you accomplish? How could you impact others? And where do you start? Now that you've heard about my magic, it's time to explore yours. Yes, you are a "magician" in your own right. Everyone possesses their own unique magic, and you are no exception.

Let's begin by defining what I mean by your magic. Your magic is the unique combination of qualities that drives you in all the magnificent things you do.

Your magic is bigger than any one activity you engage in. It's not about your job title or your bank account or your status in society. Your magic is more than these things. Your magic is limitless.

Unfortunately, sometimes we buy into the narrative that we should not take the chance of letting our magic impact anyone around us. We choose to keep it locked in a box. Thankfully, the box often has a crack or two that lets our uniqueness leak out

YOUR MAGIC IS THE UNIQUE COMBINATION OF QUALITIES THAT *DRIVES* YOU IN ALL THE MAGNIFICENT THINGS YOU DO

whether we intend it to or not. But why limit it? Why not share it every chance we get? And what stops us from sharing our magic?

There's an invisible force driven by fear and uncertainty that wants you to hide your magic, to keep it under wraps. It might even convince you that you don't know what your magic is. But if you realize how amazing you are and the potential you could unleash, perhaps you would share your magic everywhere you go, all the time, with everyone you meet.

And that is how we will close out *What Else Is Possible?* In these last few chapters, I trust you will be inspired to discover or reclaim your special magic. By describing more of the fun and amazing illusions I use in my keynotes, we will identify and reveal the true power of your magic and how to share it with others. I trust the following stories and strategies will inspire you to live life more fully while making your greatest impact.

In my keynote, I introduce what I call the Bag of Fun toward the beginning of the presentation. And by Bag of Fun, I of course mean a Target bag, which contains a few mysterious objects. What can I say? I like using ordinary props to minimize suspicion. I hand the bag to an audience member near the front row for safekeeping and ask the person to guard it and keep it closed. I then tell them we will come back to the Bag of Fun later, much as I'm going to tell you right now—we will come back to the Bag of Fun later.

Now let's turn our attention to how you can make an impact on the world around you by naming, nurturing, and sharing your unique qualities. I've boiled this down to a three-step process which I refer to as the Three Fs of Sharing Your Magic: Find It, Focus It, and Feed It. The rest of this chapter will detail how to uncover and name exactly what your special magic is, which is the first F of sharing your magic: Find It.

Step One: Find It

In order to share something, we must know what it is we are sharing. We have to search it out and recognize it when it's revealed. We have to find it.

What Your Admiration of Others Reveals

One of the best ways to discover your own magic is to recognize the unique qualities in others. So, let's do a little exercise. Start by thinking of three people you admire. They can be in your personal or professional world—you can try a variety. Any three people you hold in high regard. The first three people that come into your mind. During my keynotes I hear names of family members, friends, workmates, and even the occasional celebrity.

Now, get something to write with and something to write on, and write down those three names. You can put it as a note in your phone if that's easier. I will do this exercise right now with you. My three people are: Dan, Mike, and Deb. Do you have the names of your three people in front of you? Awesome.

Next, think of one word that represents a quality you admire about each of these people. First thing that comes to mind. It will likely be a different word for each person. Write that quality next to each of their names.

For my people, these are the qualities I have chosen:

- Dan—faith
- Mike—kindness
- Deb—generosity

Do you have your three people and a quality next to each of their names? This is important. It's best if you have these down before we go on.

At this point in my keynote, I ask for a volunteer who would like to come onto the stage to share their answers. It's obviously different for each presentation. Answers have included a family member whose quality is kindness, a friend whose strongest trait is resilience, and a coworker with exceptional leadership abilities. For this, we'll plug you into the role of volunteer, so imagine you're with me on stage and you have shared the names and qualities with the audience. Don't get stage fright now.

Consider the three qualities you admire in others. Take a hard look at those three words. Is it possible you might possess each of those qualities too? Even if just a little? Do you think people who know you well might recognize those things in you? Maybe the reason you value those traits in other people is because you know, deep down, that you possess them too. Looking at those three words may almost be like looking into a mirror of your own greatness. Even if you weren't aware of it until just now, they're the words you would be happy to hear others use to describe you. They are the things that help determine the person you are, the person you are becoming, or the person you want to become. Are you seeing that with those three words you wrote?

If you answered yes, then maybe we have already learned something about your magic. Pretty cool, isn't it?

At this point in the routine, I ask my volunteer to share which one quality excites them the most in the moment. I want you to do that now too. Go ahead and pick the one of your three words that you feel most drawn to right now. Got it? Okay, now circle or highlight the word. Say it in your head or out loud if you're alone. Just curious: What made you choose that word?

Here's my next question—do you like card tricks? Because that's what we're going to do. I'll talk you through the trick as if you're the one next to me on stage.

I have this deck of playing cards. You know what's next—pick a card, any card. Don't tell me the card. Now, I want you to use this

Sharpie to write down the word you just chose on the face of the card. Yeah, it will ruin the card, but don't worry about it. Playing cards are only about three bucks a pack and they're a business expense, so don't lose any sleep over it. But you will owe me three bucks.

Now that you've written your word on the card, put it into the pack and shuffle the cards. I love this part because typically the magician shuffles the deck. But you are shuffling the pack, which means no sleight of hand is possible here. Great shuffling skills my friend. Vegas is in your future. Now, let's put the cards back in the card box and close the lid.

Alright, time for the next prop, a brown paper bag, my most elaborate piece of equipment (not to be confused with the Bag of Fun—that's for later). *Please take the bag and make sure there is nothing inside. Empty, right? Next, the deck of cards goes into the bag, and we'll twist it at the top to keep it closed. Now for the final prop. I have this screwdriver. Didn't see that one coming, did ya?*

At this point you may be thinking—where are all these props coming from? From my prop bag, of course. Enough with the questions.

Take the screwdriver and hold it in both hands as if you're going to stab me with it. Notice I said "as if." Perfect, now check this out. You are going to impale the bag with the screwdriver. Right through the middle of the bag. Do it. Good job. Thank you for not stabbing me.

Okay, if you're imagining this in your head the way I intend, it should look a little odd. Let's recap to make sure we're on the same page, and keep in mind, you're imagining you're the person on stage with me. So, you chose a card at random and wrote your word on it. You then shuffled your card into the pack and we put the pack in the box. The card box is now in a brown paper bag that is twisted shut and impaled with a screwdriver which you are still holding. Any questions?

By the way, did you recognize the metaphor here? One of your strongest, most valuable qualities is seemingly lost. It's hidden away. Fear and uncertainty are keeping it under wraps. But you're not meant to hide your magic, you're meant to share it. That said, here comes the cool part.

Rip the screwdriver out of the side of the bag. Go ahead, do it. (Rip!). Yep, that is your card with your word impaled on the screwdriver. And yes, the rest of the cards are still in the box with the lid closed and inside the ripped bag. How did your card get on the screwdriver? How did you do that? And what is that sound, you ask? That is the sound of thunderous applause—and it's for you. Take a bow.

Before you leave the stage, I want to say this: No matter where you are or what you're doing, since that quality already lives in you and is a part of who you are, it can't help but stand out from the pack.

Uncovering Your Greater Purpose

By recognizing and celebrating those unique qualities you've been blessed with, you are already on the way to finding your magic so you can share it more fully, more often, with everyone you meet. And there is another way you can Find It. Take another look at your three words. Those three things about other people that have made a deep impression on you. What do all of those qualities have in common? If there was an overarching theme, a greater purpose, what would that be? I will expand on this idea in the context of my wonderful home life.

I love my family. We're ten people living under one roof, and watching each one share their unique magic is a never-ending education. I keep a special place in my phone notes titled "Girl Talk" where I record the funny or clever or amazing things my daughters say. I've noticed how the cute and insightful things they say can reveal deeper truths about their unique gifts and perspectives. For example, my daughter Claire has always been like a walking fortune cookie. When she was little, she used to ask things like, "Do you think there's any way you can freeze fire?" And the follow-up, "If so, would it still be hot?" I typically don't have great answers for these things. Then there was this one: "It'd be weird if I had a different dad, but then I'd say that to a different dad." And this is one of my favorites—at the age of seven, one of her deep thoughts went like this: "Daddy, if you could see through things, you wouldn't see anything at all." Whoa. Thank you, Master Yoda. You know what I can't see through? Her logic. It's solid.

And now here's a glimpse into how profound her thoughts can really be. One day when she was about ten, I was stressing about something and she said, "Worry is like quicksand. The more you worry and struggle, the quicker you sink. Just stay still, don't panic, and things will work themselves out." Talk about deep—a ten year old using a quicksand analogy for worry. You see why I write these things down.

Now, looking back on those quotes from Claire, you would see individual qualities standing out like wisdom, eloquence, and humor. In terms of an overarching theme, with those qualities combined, Claire's deepest magic might be her ability to help people see things differently.

How about you? When you think of your three words can you see a common thread? A deeper purpose? You might know immediately what it is; you can feel it inside you, maybe coming to the forefront of your mind. Or you might not know it exactly yet, but if you have even a vague sense of what it might be, don't ignore it. I invite you to write it down in your notes. Just as Claire's wisdom, eloquence, and humor at a young age were beginning to define her deeper purpose of helping others see things differently, your overarching purpose is hopefully beginning to take shape too. This is part of the magic-finding process.

While you're reflecting on that, let me give you another example. My wife Lynn has so many beautiful qualities, like love, compassion, and boldness, which are really just building blocks that point to an even greater purpose. For Lynn that's being willing to champion people to be their very best, even if it makes them temporarily uncomfortable.

As her husband, I'm one of the people she challenges the most, no matter how much I might resist. One of the areas she has called me to improve in is with my health. Many years ago, when Claire was very young, we were on a road trip and we had just eaten lunch at Gambino's Pizza in Manhattan, Kansas. Yum! After the meal, I had refilled up my cup—again—with some Dr. Pepper for the road and Claire was sipping on it in the car. Lynn said, "Devin, I want us to start eating better."

Always more than happy to push back with a little humor, I said, "Sure, let's eat better. *Better* ingredients. *Better* pizza. Papa John's." Even though I'm pretty sure that's not what she meant, I guess it all comes down to pizza for me. I mean, have you tried Papa John's garlic butter sauce? Oh my goodness. I put it all over everything. I even use it like essential oils and put it all over my body (I don't really—or do I?).

Anyway, one day, Lynn made some asparagus for dinner.

"Ew, why?" I said.

"They've done studies, Devin. Asparagus is proven to improve your memory."

Guess I forgot. But it's true. I ate some and then remembered stuff. I was like, "Oh yeah—I have a gag reflex."

It was a hard process, and yes, I gave a lot of pushback. But she inspired me to get healthier, and in the end, I gained confidence and strength and became a better example for my kids. I also lost a significant amount of weight. Maybe Lynn is the real magician—she made fifty pounds disappear!

Lynn sharing her magic with me, even in just this one area, changed my life and our family forever. The same thing can happen when you share your magic with the world, even if it's just one person at a time.

The Power of Recalling Past Success

But here's where it can really get challenging. Sometimes our minds can trick us into believing that our magic isn't enough to make a meaningful impact. You may question if you can really make the difference you've been called to create or become the person you truly want to be.

Have you ever felt that way?

In my keynote I ask for a volunteer who feels some uncertainty about one of the characteristics from their list of three words. Someone who would love to embody that trait with more confidence. It could be leadership, positivity, talent, or any of many characteristics that make us who we are.

Since you did such an amazing job with the card trick, let's bring you back to the stage for an encore.

Which of your three traits would you like to really live out at home, work, and in your community but are having a hard time fully demonstrating? Go ahead and name out loud the quality you would love to embody with more unshakable confidence and clarity. Now, a few questions about that:

- *What would be possible if you fully embodied this quality?*
- *Is it conceivable that you are already embodying this quality more than you realize?*
- *Even if you feel out of touch with it now, can you reflect on a time when you successfully embodied this quality? Maybe once or multiple times? Can you think of a specific time you embodied it, even if just a little? Take a second to think about this before moving on.*
- *In that situation, how did you successfully demonstrate this quality? Your answer can be as detailed or big pictured as you want.*

Now, imagine the feeling of this quality growing exponentially as you give it your full attention. This part of the magic finding and reclaiming process is vital because when you recognize the magic you already have, you can realize how rich it really is. That is when it can come alive for you.

Isn't it interesting to notice that perhaps you have embodied this quality before, even if just a little? And see how noticing it can make you feel different, maybe even more confident, in this moment? How do you feel? Great, I hope. In psychology, this is known as positive autobiographical memory recall, which basically means that actively remembering past successes can boost your confidence to take on new challenges. Remember that you can tap into this feeling any time. Pretty cool, huh?

I have one last question for you—do you have any cash on you? A $100 bill. Perfect. Can we use that to illustrate something about your quality? Before you hand it to me, let's make sure you can identify it at any time as yours. Take this Sharpie and write your name on the bill. Great, now go ahead and hand it to me.

So, what are we doing here? Well, this bill has value just like that specific quality you named. I want to use this bill to demonstrate how to hold onto that quality by being aware of what could get in the way.

Your perception of that quality is what's going to make it alive for you. And if I fold this bill in half several times, notice your perception is that it gets smaller and smaller, even though the value is still the same. So, what can threaten us from fully seeing our value? One word. Burnout.

(Now, envision me pulling a lighter out of my pocket, lighting your money on fire, and watching it vanish in a bright ball of fire.)

Awesome, huh? Want to see it again? Give me another $100 bill. You don't want to? Oh, I know why—because it seems like your money is gone. And it is—for now. Burnout can make it seem like our magic has evaporated into thin air.

And what do I mean by burnout? It could be anything from not getting enough sleep, to skipping exercise, to never giving yourself a real break. But when you recognize the early signs and take action to prevent burnout, not only can you reclaim your magic—you might even be surprised by how quickly it returns.

And speaking of surprises . . .

Please go and grab the Bag of Fun from our amazing helper.

(That's right—it's the big Bag of Fun moment you've been waiting for.)

Hand it to me. Thanks. Inside here are two things—this knife and this lemon. I will cut all the way around the middle of the lemon. There we go. Now, I'll hold this half of the lemon, and you grab the other half and let's twist it apart. Well, look at that. It looks like some folded up money is sticking out of the middle of the fruit. Pull that out of there and unfold it. Hm, looks like a $100 bill, but no way could that be your bill—that would be impossible. Only one way to know for sure—is that your name in your handwriting? You better believe it is!

As amazing as that was, remember this: The money in this fruit is nothing compared to the valuable surprises waiting inside of you.

So, once you have found or reclaimed your magic, the next question is—what do you do with it?

What else is possible?

CHAPTER NINE

Share Your Magic

ONCE YOU GET a handle on your brand of magic, it's time to have some real fun. Time to lean into the process of further defining and caring for your magic in order to best share it with the world. The next step is to Focus It. When I say Focus It, I don't mean zeroing in on any particular activity, but more importantly, focusing on your greater purpose.

Step Two: Focus It

As a child, I was focusing on my greater purpose without even realizing it. From the early days of watching several magicians perform, I began admiring qualities in others that I more deeply wanted to express, like dedication, resilience, and passion. And that sparked a greater purpose in me—to wow people. To create the kinds of responses I get when the money appears inside the fruit.

I started to focus on exploring anything I could learn or do to achieve a wow factor. Things like soccer juggling, drums (more specifically, marching snare), and piano (to illustrate this in my keynotes, I often become a one-man talent show and display these skills). But ultimately I found that magic was the thing that wowed people the most, so I decided to pour everything I had into developing my craft as a magician and presenter. I decided to Focus It. And that's what I did when I was about eighteen years old. Focus in a way that I never had before.

Around that time, I paid a regular visit to U. S. Toy (the place with the magic shop I mentioned earlier), and a magician there showed me a trick that completely amazed me. It was unlike any other magic trick I had ever seen. And this was especially significant because of how I had been feeling at the time—uninspired and unmotivated. In those days, my interest in magic would have peaks and valleys. For a period of time I would eat, sleep, and breathe magic, but other times I would go months without touching a deck of cards. I would even question if I had fallen out of love with magic, this thing I had once been so passionate about.

But when the magician in the shop showed me this trick, it immediately reignited that excitement and passion, and it reminded me of how I could make people feel when I was performing mind-blowing magic. So, I was inspired to master the trick myself.

If you are in a creative job or even in your more creative hobbies, do you ever find it difficult to continually tap into that energy? Have you been in a place where you really needed some sort of lightning bolt to get you moving once again? Some person or other inspiration to propel you toward further success? Something to cause you to ask, *What else is possible?* This experience in the magic shop was my lightning bolt. And by the way—what was the trick and who was the magician? Remember the coin teleportation trick I described earlier that, as it turns out, was possible without the cover of the playing cards? This was the one, and the magician was none other than the mastermind behind the moves, John B. Born.

This trick was part of the inspiration that led me to devote time, effort, and resources to magic in a way I had never done with anything else before. And I learned that when you pour yourself into something and keep putting new things out there, other people start to take notice. You read earlier how a casting agent from *America's Got Talent* personally reached out to ask me to audition for the show because they were so impressed by my online magic videos.

But here's a part of the story you haven't heard. There was one genre of magic in particular that caught their attention. It's known as "pickpocket entertainment." In a nutshell, pickpocket entertainment is what happens when a magician performs a trick while temporarily, secretly "stealing" something valuable from an audience member without the participant knowing. If all goes as planned and the subject is unaware the magician has made the "lift," their reaction of shock is priceless when they are handed back their valuables. It's all for entertainment. Like I mentioned earlier, I used to practice this on campus at Johnson County Community College.

As a fun sidenote: The moment I successfully lifted that first watch all those years ago, I was hooked. After a while, I couldn't help but notice other people's watches. Was it a Timex? A Rolex? Did it fasten with Velcro or a buckle? I became a student of watches, particularly the clasps. Over time, I virtually mastered the ability to instantly identify the clasp type with just a quick glance at the watch face. Pretty good, right? My internal monologue would go something like this: *Oh, that one would be easy to take. If I could just shake hands with that person, I'd be home free.* It became a feat I could pull off with success pretty much every time I tried.

And of all the kinds of magic I've learned, this is hands down the most difficult. But I was driven to do it because it had the ultimate mind-blowing effect on participants and audience members. And when the talent recruiters at AGT saw it online, they were impressed. Not just that, but in an effort to stay new and fresh, they had decided that for season nine they specifically wanted a "pickpocket entertainer." Even with all the videos of my magic and mentalism they might have seen, this is what they were drawn to, mainly because it was unique to them. So, this was great timing for me to be a "pickpocket," and if I hadn't focused on my pick-pocketing skills, I might not have had that incredible opportunity to go to Hollywood and audition.

The Great Masquerade

Here's another part of the AGT story you don't know. That ex-perience taught me more than just what it means to rise through failure and the resiliency of Picking Up the Ball. And it taught me more than the importance of Always Giving Thanks. It taught me an even deeper principle—something profound—about my magic. You see, during all my years of performing, I thought I had been so clear and focused on my purpose. After the AGT experience, though, I had to really question whether that was true or not. I had a realization that the things that had been partly driving me to perform all those years were fears and insecurities masquer-ading as my purpose.

Maybe you can relate to this. Have you ever been going along, experiencing success in something, and realized your motivations are not quite right? You've made it all about you? I know I did. My desire to "wow" people with magic was less about them and more about me. Performing had ultimately become about the desire to impress. I realized I was striving to be found worthy by other people; clinging to the need for compliments and approval. And if I didn't get that positive feedback, I'd become slightly depressed. Or I would lose focus and interest in magic. And when the acco-lades didn't come on *America's Got Talent*—the moment I thought would change everything—I felt worthless.

THE THINGS THAT HAD BEEN PARTLY DRIVING ME TO PERFORM ALL THOSE YEARS WERE FEARS *AND* INSECURITIES MASQUERADING AS MY PURPOSE

The True Meaning of M.A.G.I.C.

Have things like fear or insecurity ever hijacked your magic and transformed something you once loved into something self-focused and pressure-filled? Did that something you once loved become about attempting to prove your worth or make that one activity into your whole identity? What if there is something you can do to reclaim your purpose, your magic? Good news—there is. And it's all about focus. When you are doing anything from a place of neediness and insecurity, it can make things so heavy that you may want to quit altogether. That's where this new frame of mind comes in. *It's not about me, it's about them.* In other words, my magic tricks are a vehicle to bless others. Not impress others. It's about the audience I'm in front of, wherever I happen to be performing. Once I refocused and realized my gifts are primarily a vehicle to bless other people, things started changing (it's poetry time again) . . .

> *When I made the shift from impress to bless,*
> *I went from feeling worthless to priceless,*
> *Purposeless to marvelous.*
> *I went from being bored to being on board,*
> *Because what I was missin' was a greater mission,*
> *To take me from losing traction to choosing action.*
> *And most importantly,*
> *I went from feeling deficient to feeling magnificent.*

Remember how I said your magic is made up of the unique qualities that drive you in all the magnificent things you do? Well, focusing that *magnificence* in a way that *generously* serves others is where things get truly magical. Because what is magic really, but magnificence and generosity in combination.

Did you catch that? M-A-G-I-C is . . .

Magnificence
And
Generosity
In
Combination

Step Three: Feed It

First you have to find your magic, then focus on your greater purpose. But how can you share this kind of magic, your real magic, more fully, more of the time? This brings us to the third F—you have to Feed It. Feed It as in "feeding" it to others, meaning to share your magic joyfully and without expectation, including in situations that may initially feel like you're sabotaging greater possibilities for yourself.

"Alright Stop, Collaborate, and Listen"

I know, I know—best section title ever. And while Vanilla Ice probably didn't intend for his lyrics to inspire a mindset shift, that word *"collaborate"* hit me differently later in life.

One big hurdle to sharing your magic often shows up when it feels like you might be feeding your competition. That can lead to things like holding back from referring your "archrival" to a buyer when you're unavailable—even when you know they offer an amazing service. Or maybe you choose not to share helpful ideas with competitors, like a new piece of software or a more efficient system.

Confession time: Once, another magician complimented my business cards and asked who made them, and I wouldn't tell him. I guess I wanted to protect my title as the magician with the best-looking business cards in town. Ridiculous! Eventually, I decided to stop, listen . . . and actually embrace the *collaborate* part. I gave him the name of the vendor, and thankfully, we now laugh about the whole situation.

If you notice even a hint of hesitation around collaboration, I encourage you to reframe your thinking here.

Cavett Robert, founder of the National Speakers Association, said with regards to the competitive element of speaking, "Don't worry about how we divide up the pie. There is enough for everybody. Let's just make a bigger pie!"

John F. Kennedy said, "A rising tide lifts all boats."

A quote often attributed to James Keller states, "A candle loses nothing by lighting another candle."

These wise messages make so much sense. The more we collaborate, the better things are for everyone. It's counterintuitive, but generously feeding others in turn feeds you.

When I first started in magic, if a request came in for a date I was unavailable, I was hesitant to recommend another magician to fill the slot. I didn't want a potential client to hire one of my competitors and risk losing their business moving forward. I wanted them to assume I was the only option they had. I hoped they would be so disappointed they couldn't land a magician that they would book me immediately for next year's event. This was obviously a glaring symptom of my insecurity at that time. It was a mentality of scarcity.

Then I began to see that if I gave a recommendation for another magician, eventually that competitor would, in turn, pass the word on about me. The same was true when I started working with speakers. The predominant culture with this group is give, give, give. Back to Cavett Robert's idea: Don't fight for a piece of the pie—help everyone make a bigger pie. Even if someone who was going to book me finds another speaker who aligns better with their message, or they simply prefer his or her style over mine, that's no reason to panic. There is plenty of work out there for all of us.

Making a bigger pie in the speaking world looks like becoming my best as a presenter to reflect well on the profession and help maintain a positive impression in general for speakers in the minds of meeting professionals. It means helping, learning from, and referring fellow speakers, because as the old proverb says, "As iron sharpens iron, so one person sharpens another." In fact, just this morning, I booked an engagement that my speaker friend referred me for because he was already booked. We both book engagements regularly by referring each other. Making a bigger pie also involves demonstrating to event planners that it would serve them well to continue booking good speakers because there are so many talented people out there. It involves educating meeting organizers who have never hired a speaker that we can bring a new level of inspiration and fun to their conferences. It's a mentality of abundance and possibility that helps me live in a giving, loving, secure way. How can *you* make a bigger "pie" for the people in your circles?

These days, I genuinely want the best for my competitors. But I'll admit, it takes daily effort and prayer to stay in this mindset. My naturally selfish tendencies often clash with my deeper desire to lead with unconditional love and generosity.

Letting go of the illusion of control—over situations, opportunities, and people—has been incredibly freeing. When I was stuck in a competitive mindset, I was spinning my wheels, draining my energy, and ultimately holding myself back. In trying to protect my connections and opportunities, I was unknowingly shutting myself off from even greater ones. I thought I was making life easier, but in reality, I was only making it harder.

Looking back, I see how much time and energy I wasted guarding things I should have been freely giving. But when I shifted to sharing my magic, doors began to open—doors I never could have unlocked in a mindset of self-preservation and fear. Now, one of my greatest desires is to bless others from the abundance of my own blessings.

I have tried to apply this mentality to all aspects of my business, even when it's uncomfortable.

Magician Todd Lamanske is someone I used to view as my biggest competitor, even though we've been great friends for twenty years strong. I'll be honest, old habits of the scarcity mindset and my competitive nature made me hesitate including his full name here in my book. Crazy, right? Todd was the one who wanted the business card vendor's name. Sure, Todd has been a competitor over the years. I've lost some gigs to him and vice versa. But, since I've pivoted to speaking and his primary focus is still magic, we have little overlap with potential buyers (even though we're in the same market). Regardless, there are times I am able to cover for him when he's in a pinch and he can do the same for me. The fact that I started viewing him as a collaborator over a competitor has resulted in so much good for both of us.

For example, Todd has been at the magic game longer than me and is a more committed student of magic in general, so along with being my good friend, I also like to think of him as my unofficial magic consultant. He is instrumental in helping me develop and perfect many of the jaw-dropping tricks I am using today in my keynotes. I mean why not—even David Copperfield collaborates with other magicians! But of course, the brainstorming goes both ways, and our relationship really is a major win-win. This sense of teamwork has only deepened our connection and made our times together that much more enjoyable. I treasure our friendship.

What about you? Are there opportunities to partner with others? When it comes to sharing your magic, how can you Feed It by empowering your so-called "competitors," turning them into collaborators and creating more win-win possibilities?

First-Class Magic

Feeding It, of course, doesn't only apply to business. It's a way of life. Generously sharing your magic can happen anytime, anywhere, in any kind of setting. It might even happen on an airplane.

I don't know about you, but when I'm traveling I often keep to myself. This might not be obvious, but I'm an introvert. When I'm flying, I've learned that if I take a little time to recharge while I'm in the air, I can be more present for others when the plane lands. That means I'm more likely to listen to a podcast or watch a movie, although every so often I do still get lost in a good conversation. And then sometimes my solitude gets completely disrupted, like this one time when I was traveling to a performance in Canada.

After I had just boarded the plane and sat down, the flight attendant, Julie, was enthusiastically greeting each passenger. Three words I would use to describe Julie are outgoing, cheerful, and inviting. As you're about to find out, those three qualities work together to reveal Julie's deeper magic: inspiring others to share *their* magic. She really broke me out of my shell and inspired me to show up differently. I was seated near the rear of the plane and decided that if she made it back to my seat, I would do something special for her in return. I would "steal" her watch.

Just after the plane had finished boarding and everyone was settling in, Julie stopped by my seat and happened to ask the perfect question: "What do you do for a living?"

I said, "Hold out your hands and I'll show you." I guess she'd never heard that one because she gave me a weird look. Then I explained that I'm a magician and asked if she'd like to see a trick. That didn't seem to make things less weird—shocker—but even so, she said sure. I took out some half dollars and started doing sleight of hand with the coins, making them jump "invisibly" from one of her hands to the other. She thought it was pretty cool. This was just a distraction, because of course, in the meantime, I had stolen her watch.

Keep in mind: When I perform a watch steal, I always give it back when I like the person. No I'm kidding—I always give it back.

I finished the coin trick and was about to make the big reveal, when suddenly Julie realized she needed to make an announcement and headed to the very back of the plane. That's when I took a closer look at the watch. It was a Rolex. Oops. I had thought it was a Timex. *This is worth way more*, I thought. *More jail time.* No, just kidding. At least I hoped I was kidding.

Then I decided this could be really fun. Some of the people around me had been watching the trick, so I showed them the watch and they couldn't believe it. I said, "Let's mess with Julie a little bit. Check this out." I held her watch up in the air and just let it dangle from my fingertips, and we were all on the edge of our seats waiting for her to notice.

I was sitting about five or six seats from the back of the plane, just a little ways in front of where she was making her announcement. She picked up the intercom phone-thingy (that's its official name) and said, "Good afternoon, ladies and gentlemen! Welcome to Delta! Today we are headed to Saksatoon. We hope that you . . . *is that my watch*?" She really projected those last words. It was definitely the most unprofessional announcement I'd ever heard on an airplane. Every head on the plane turned simultaneously as she stared at me with her mouth hanging wide open, doing double takes of both the watch and her bare wrist.

She quickly wrapped up her announcement and *very* quickly walked up to my seat to get a closer look at the watch. Sometimes I joke that she was angry, but she actually took it really well and was laughing and being playful. Don't you love when people get it? She said, "How did you get that off my wrist?"

I could only answer with, "I think you dropped these." Then I handed back her pen and notepad, which I had also lifted during the coin trick. Her jaw fell open again, then she grabbed her belongings and walked off to the front of the plane to continue her work, still laughing in disbelief. She was such a joy and would be a *perfect* helper on stage for a pickpocket routine.

As the people around me were laughing together and asking me all kinds of questions about my abilities and profession and criminal record (joking, joking!), I quickly realized I had definitely sacrificed my introvert time. And I was okay with that—this was way worth it.

Okay, now fast-forward a few minutes; we're all buckled up, about to take off. The first-class curtain pops open, and Julie comes power walking back to me. "Hey, Devin." This can't be good, right? She knows my name, kind of like how teachers only know the unruly kids' names on the first day of school. "A seat just opened in first class. Do you want it?"

Looking back, I probably should've been more worried at that moment, with thoughts like: *Are you putting me by the air marshal?* or *Will the Royal Canadian Mounted Police be waiting for me on their horses when we land?* Nah, only kidding. I knew there had to be a kind, meaningful reason behind her gesture—so I asked her why she gave me the upgrade.

She simply said, "Because you made my day."

The thought of it still makes me smile.

Now, there are three things I would like to highlight about this story:

First, did you notice who shared their magic before anyone else? Julie did, which prompted me. This shows you that when you are the first to share your magic, no matter how new or scary it might seem, you can encourage others to do the same.

Second, did you notice the magic routine that fell flat in my AGT audition is the same routine that wowed Julie that day on the airplane? This goes to show that just because your magic isn't well received in one setting doesn't mean it won't be a home run in another. So keep sharing.

And third, when you make sharing your magic a lifestyle, you can inspire others in ways you may not have imagined. And if you remember to Find It, Focus It, and Feed It, you might even find yourself flying through life first class.

What else is possible?

CHAPTER TEN

The Blessing of Imperfection

WHO ARE YOU called to share your magic with? Are there people at work or at home who are counting on you to get up every day and do what you were born to do? Who motivates you to get out of bed with a smile; who makes your life worth living?

When I consider these questions, my family comes to mind as what's most valuable. I have eight kids who look to me for guidance, love, and consistency. They think I'm the best dad ever—I even have a "Best Dad Ever" mug to prove it. No, I didn't pull a Michael Scott and buy the mug for myself; it was a Father's Day gift. But come on, am I *actually* the best dad ever? Yes, I am—to my daughters, because I'm *their* dad!

Today, our family roll call looks a lot like the von Trapp's. I don't have a whistle like the captain, but I want one. As I've already mentioned, the oldest, Claire, is sixteen. Charlotte is fourteen, Cambry is eleven, Elsie is nine, Eva is six, Emme is four, Haven is two, and Ivy is the one-month-old newest addition. I'm guessing on some of those—I'm not good with names (ha!). Lots of princess dresses and My Little Pony toys adorn our home, and I absolutely love raising a house full of daughters.

Being a top-notch keynote speaker is my goal every workday, but being a top-notch husband and father drives every waking and sleeping thought. In fact, I strive for perfection.

Perfection Is Not an Option

But am I perfect? Get ready for this bombshell—no, I'm not. Let's just say, family life offers endless opportunities to witness imperfection in action—and I'm usually leading the charge.

Here are a few fun examples of what I mean by perfection not being an option. Have you ever texted someone, but you didn't check the message before you sent it? If you have clumsy thumbs, not only can you confuse a person, you can potentially ruin a relationship. One of my best texting errors was the time I was home with all the kids, and my wife was away for a much-deserved break. I intended to send her this text:

The kids are missing you.

But somehow, I cut off the word "you," which *really* changes the message.

You know what she texted back? A smiley-face emoji and two thumbs up. I wasn't completely sure if she was smiling about my error or the "missing kids." Did I mention Lynn has a great sense of humor? Perfection is not an option, and a huge part of what has kept our family strong and connected are the endless opportunities to extend and receive grace when we make mistakes.

I love being a family man and I wouldn't trade it for anything in the world, but letting people get close can be vulnerable and humbling at times. For example, have you ever gotten feedback from a coworker or family member that stung a little? Well, kids can be *brutally* honest. Sometimes they're not even intending to hurl insults—it just happens.

One time when one of my daughters was around seven years old, she said out of nowhere, "Hey Dad, you have a big nose."

I said, "Well, it's genetic. So, in your face. Literally." A sense of humor goes a long way when you have a child with no filter to point out all your flaws.

And then sometimes they accidentally insult me simply because of their wording. One time as I was leaving for an ugly Christmas sweater party, one of my daughters said, "Good luck at the ugly festival. I know you'll win." Hey, she's confident in my ugliness. Apparently I don't even need the sweater—my natural ugliness is more than enough.

Another time, one of them said, "Dad, you need to look more like Zac Efron." I've been trying, but that hasn't been working out so well.

I wanted to share these examples because they're entertaining: They're silly examples of how perfection is not an option. But in all seriousness, sometimes the feedback we receive can really hurt. So, I'm also sharing these examples as a reminder that when we're willing to persevere through all of life's imperfections, we're oftentimes rewarded in ways that surprise us. These surprises make you feel like maybe you're doing something right.

This happened one time when we had only three kids—Cambry was an infant, Charlotte was a two-year-old, and Claire, our oldest, was five. It was the end of what felt like a really long day, I was completely exhausted, and I had come home and crashed on the bed.

Even though I was extremely tired, my mind started racing as I looked back on the day, thinking about all that goes into being a parent and how I was feeling imperfect, to say the least. At that moment, I was wondering whether or not I truly had what it took to be a parent. I asked myself questions like, *How in the world am I going to get up tomorrow and do this all again?* Do you ever feel that way? At the same time another part of me was saying, *Am I even doing enough?* and *Have I made mistakes as a parent that I can't recover from?* And right then, Claire, five years old, walked in the room and snuggled up next to me. I put my arms around her, and she said, "Daddy, you make me feel safe."

Suddenly, all the worries and stresses melted away, and my greater purpose was the only thing that mattered. That moment was priceless—an instant of pure connection. It taught me something profound about life in general: Enduring the imperfect moments is what helps make the perfect ones possible.

Remodeling My Mindset

Perfectionism has shadowed me my whole life, and I've often had unreasonably high expectations of those around me. But in recent years, I've been trying to shed my tendencies to micromanage. Can you relate? One of the ways I recently attempted this was by asking Lynn to manage the project of our two bathroom remodels. It was something I didn't have the capacity to take on at the time, so I told her I was good with her making all the decisions. She did a great job, calling the shots on everything from vanities to shower heads, with the exception of asking my opinion every now and then. Long story short, one bathroom is all pink, but it's alright—the girls love it. Okay—so do I.

Maybe you've heard of the Pygmalion effect, which Wikipedia defines as "a psychological phenomenon in which high expectations lead to improved performance in a given area and low expectations lead to worse performance." Perhaps there is some truth in that; nonetheless, I made a conscious decision to lower my expectations for this project. I just knew for me, had I

ENDURING THE *IMPERFECT* MOMENTS IS WHAT HELPS MAKE THE PERFECT ONES POSSIBLE

maintained those high expectations, they would have slowly transitioned from reasonable to unreasonable in nature, and that wouldn't have been fun for anyone.

I was making the conscious and intentional decision to match my expectations with more realistic possible outcomes. I was restraining myself from attempting to force everything to turn out the way I thought it should, and instead, appreciating the beauty when it didn't.

I knew the bathrooms wouldn't turn out to be perfect, but they did turn out to be beautiful. I was sure Lynn wouldn't always pick things I would prefer. There were choices she made along the way, and I was like, *Oh, really?* But then I reminded myself I had trusted her with it and couldn't, or at least *shouldn't*, complain. She saved me countless hours of decision-making, conversations with the remodelers, and Home Depot runs. The process was not always as smooth as we would have liked, and we actually ran into one huge problem (not her fault), but in the end it was worth it. It didn't turn out exactly like I thought it would, but it helped me grow as a person in relinquishing perfectionism and surrendering control. It freed me up to write this book, work on my keynote, learn some new illusions, make strides on my podcast, and spend more time with my kids. The truth is, even if I had micromanaged the entire remodel, there still would have been problems—likely more.

Business and Imperfection: The Great Merge

In my line of work, I interact with event planners on a regular basis. I don't know how they do it. If anyone knows perfection is not an option, it's event planners. There are so many areas where they need to pay attention and so many things that can go wrong. The sound system can go out, their keynote speaker may miss a connecting flight—never me, of course (insert nervous laughter and the sound of knocking on wood)—or the caterer might get stuck in traffic. At a recent event I spoke at, the breakfast was so late that the tables hadn't been cleared by the time lunch was served. Perfection is not an option no matter how much you plan. From what I've seen in all my years of speaking, the demeanor of the event planner in the midst of imperfection is a huge determining factor for how everyone else will respond to the curve balls being thrown. The best event planners I've worked with don't tend to complain, have a good sense of humor, and maintain a positive attitude, no matter what.

If you work in an office, no doubt you're aware your environment will never be perfect. There might be too much noise, especially if you work next to someone like Milton from *Office Space*. ("I was told that I could listen to the radio at a reasonable volume from nine to eleven.") You might not always love the temperature, the people, or the smell (hopefully those last two things aren't related). Rather than allowing factors out of our control to cause us stress, it's much more productive to focus on managing the things that are *within* our control.

It seems one of my niches as a speaker has been presenting to companies going through mergers. These groups are in a perfect place to be asking, *What else is possible?* When companies merge, things can be less than perfect, to say the least. You may lose teammates you trusted, an office with a view, some perks you had always relied on, or a culture you came to love. And if you're trying to converge strategic goals and core values, good luck coming up with lists that will be acceptable, let alone perfect, in everyone's eyes. But what possibilities lie ahead! The most seamless and successful mergers happen when individuals don't let their former expectations get in the way of the beauty that can come from a newfound collaboration with others who are equally motivated to create something greater together.

It took me a long time to learn that we have the choice and opportunity to take advantage of imperfection, including when we perceive it in others. I have witnessed my fellow speakers and entertainers make mistakes in business and on stage that have saved me a lot of grief from learning the same lessons firsthand. I also hope others benefit from watching *my* missteps.

Perfection is not an option, and we can be thankful for that, because *imperfection* is a blessing. It keeps you growing, keeps you learning, keeps you thinking. Imperfection sparks creativity, strengthens collaboration, and consistently reminds us that something greater is always possible.

Pointing to Your "Rope Pullers"

One of the greatest tools to help alleviate a less-than-perfect life is the regular practice of celebration.

Remember the "Daddy, you make me feel safe" moment when Claire was five? Okay, now fast-forward ten years. Claire was fifteen and had made the cast of a local production of *The Wizard of Oz*, which was perfect because we live in Kansas.

Claire asked if I would help out with the production. I said, "Absolutely. What will I be doing exactly?"

And she said, "Well, our director . . . she said you look strong."

"Go on," I said with the suave of Hugh Jackman, or at least I hoped.

"We're going to have witches and monkeys flying around, and we need parents backstage to pull the ropes."

I thought, *Wow, they're going all out; it's going to be like a full-on Broadway-style production.* I said, "I'm in."

Little did I know how serious my job was about to become. We had a trainer. When you have a trainer, that may mean there's an element of danger involved. On the first day, I asked the trainer a question that changed everything: "What if you have a kid up in the air, and you let go of the rope? I mean by accident, of course."

She said, "If you let go, they'll fall."

"How fast?" I was thinking there must be some kind of built-in safety feature that slows the person's twenty-foot fall to the ground to prevent a serious injury. I was wrong.

The trainer said, "They would fall at the speed of gravity." Well, I was glad we didn't breeze by that tiny detail.

All of a sudden, I realized two things: One, how crucial it is that I pay very close attention during the training, and two, I was glad *I* was the one holding my daughter's rope, because nobody could hold it tighter. I decided to face the challenge head-on, even though we were a bunch of amateur parents who had never done anything like this before. Pulling off a safe and amazing production together was our seemingly impossible goal.

If the parents pulling the ropes did our jobs right, we would make onstage magic. Glinda the Good Witch floating in her bubble, the Wicked Witch of the West speeding around on her broomstick, not to mention the flying monkeys and then the whole tornado scene.

The only problem was, we couldn't *start ugly* (as in Start Ugly, Start Small, Pick Up the Ball) because this was a "safety is our highest priority" kind of situation with no room for error. You can drop the ball, but you cannot drop the kid. This is one of those instances in life in which we knew we needed to temporarily abandon the "perfection is not an option" mindset and embrace the discipline that "failure is not an option." This mentality is a given for high-risk industries with risk-averse cultures. Just ask loggers, surgeons, and pilots, among other like-minded professions.

Here's the kicker—we had to become "fly masters" in just three days, meaning that's the length of time the trainer would be present, after which we would be left on our own. I'll never forget pulling the ropes for Claire for the first time after the trainer was gone. No more supervision. Moment of truth. Had I paid close enough attention? I sure hoped so.

Claire played the character of Miss Gulch, who is the witch character before she becomes the Wicked Witch. Her rigging with the ropes was one of the more intricate and therefore dangerous setups. She was on a bicycle, in a "tornado," twenty feet in the air! This is my baby we're talking about. As far as I was concerned, she was still five years old. I recalled her sweet words, "Daddy, you make me feel safe," and I wanted her to maintain that sentiment.

After just a few days of manning the ropes without the trainer present and several successful practice runs, we started the actual performances. I was telling everyone, "Whatever you do—don't tell me to break a leg."

In the end, despite my concerns for everyone's safety and how many things could have gone wrong, we pulled off six incredible and safe performances. And while we knew total perfection was not an option, safety was of course our first priority. The well-being of the students was at stake, so every time we put someone up in the air, we put all of our focus into ensuring we followed the trainer's instructions to a T. We achieved a seemingly impossible goal, and it took the full participation of every single person on the rope-pulling team. We were encouraging and supporting each other all along the way. Sometimes we had to pull the rope for someone else because they were called away to repair a prop or fix someone's microphone. This means we were constantly *picking up the ball* for each other. After each "flight," we celebrated with lots of fist bumps.

I was slowly discovering that a culture of celebration was a vital part of this theater company's success. More than I ever would have guessed.

On the first night, something happened that totally surprised me. At the conclusion of the play, during the curtain call just after they took their bow, the students did something really cool. They turned and all together pointed backstage, and I realized that *point* was to us—everyone helping behind the scenes.

I was doing the work simply because I love my daughter. I wasn't expecting any special recognition, and I think that was part of what made it feel so good—that it was an *unexpected* show of appreciation. The "we couldn't have done this without you" message was loud and clear and resonated with me deeply. The students repeated this sentiment at the conclusion of every show.

For me, working "behind the scenes" was only a week-long endeavor. If no one had appreciated me or I hadn't gotten the point after each performance, I can't imagine it would have made me bitter, for a lack of better words. But when I think about people who work a job "behind the scenes" day in and day out, year after year after year, without the regular or even occasional show of appreciation, I can imagine this would make a person less and less passionate about the work they do over time.

It just so happens that oftentimes there are many behind-the-scenes "rope pullers" in my audiences when I speak. These people are the unsung heroes of the organization, such as administrative professionals, I.T., and other support staff. I regularly speak to school districts for annual convocations or all-staff meetings. For one such keynote, after what I felt was a very successful presentation, I was reading the feedback comments from the attendees. All of the comments were positive up until the very end, when I came across this one:

> [*Devin's program was*] *Aimed at the majority (teachers); however, all classified staff were present and not mentioned or included. However, everyone works together within the district to make the students' lives better.*

Ouch. For me, but more so for *them*. Now, I know I mentioned the words "support staff" at least a time or two in that particular presentation, thinking I had covered my bases. However, it didn't seem to matter. Honorable mentions are great, but sometimes it takes more. Apparently, I was aiming most of my content toward the teachers, which made this individual feel insignificant. The fact that I so drastically underemphasized the importance of these key people made at least one of them feel *completely* unnoticed.

Well, guess what? Now when speaking to school districts, or any organization for that matter, I do my best to ensure that *everyone* feels appreciated and connected to my content. Part of this means I do my homework beforehand to determine how to best balance my customization of the message and address the support staff when possible. This means when I'm speaking at conferences, I've been known to pay special attention to vendors, sponsors, event planners, and even the A/V team running sound and production, pulling the ropes behind the scenes and creating all the magic on the front end. It does mean I must be more intentional and aware, but it's way worth the extra time and effort to make these people feel seen.

Leaders of the most successful organizations I have worked with tell me that the best way to attract and retain better quality talent is to regularly show gratitude and appreciation. Positive psychology studies consistently show that people who regularly show and receive gratitude are more engaged, productive, happy, and optimistic. And a great thing about this is that it costs nothing to simply tell people they matter, they're doing a great job, and the organization wouldn't operate properly without their efforts.

How about you? Are you working backstage—behind the scenes in your personal or professional life—pulling ropes others don't even see? And are the people on the other end of those ropes showing you the appreciation you deserve? I hope so. But if not, here's a powerful shift: become a pointer.

Make it a habit to call out the great work of others. Celebrate them. Go out of your way to shine a light on the ones making things happen. You might be surprised how often that appreciation circles back to you. And if it doesn't? You'll still be known as someone who built a legacy of lifting others up. What better reason to be praised—than for being someone who regularly praises others?

And here's the next question: Who's pulling the ropes in your life and work? Who's behind the curtain, making your success possible? Maybe it's your manager, your mechanic, or your mom. Whoever it is—have you pointed to them lately? Imagine how the world would change if we all took a moment to recognize the ones who keep things running. Why not start today?

Even the teenagers from that *Wizard of Oz* cast knew that to accomplish greater things together, one of the simplest things we can do is celebrate each other. I'm talking about always giving thanks, but this time, to the people around you.

Mix, Match, and Win

How about one more trick before we wrap things up? It's currently how I close my keynote. I'm going to describe this illusion not only to make you scratch your head, but to serve as a reminder that, even in the face of imperfection, greater possibilities are always in store for you.

Here's how the trick goes: I present two well-mixed Rubik's Cubes and invite a random volunteer from the audience to the stage. I always ask the person if they have experience solving the puzzle, and most people claim they have either never solved one or can only solve one side. They typically don't know what most Rubik's Cube enthusiasts know: that the number of different possible combinations with a Rubik's Cube is over forty-three quintillion, which is forty-three followed by eighteen zeros. As you're about to find out, this fact makes the trick more impressive.

I place one cube down on a table in full view of the audience (this is important for later). I hand the other cube over and give the volunteer the seemingly impossible goal of solving the cube successfully in thirty seconds or less—with their eyes closed.

By the way, are you ever handed a "puzzle" at home or at the office that looks impossible to figure out? You feel like your eyes are closed and you can't see what's next. Do you ask what the point is when a situation presents itself and it appears you will be wasting time trying to make things work? People are watching you and maybe even judging you—wondering what in the world you are doing. Should you quit? Should you walk away? Well, I suggest you have a little faith, ask *what else is possible*, and see what happens.

With eyes closed, the volunteer begins randomly twisting the cube. I say to the audience, "Now, since I've given her very little time, her eyes are closed, *and* her chances are roughly one in forty-three quintillion, you're probably thinking, 'This ain't gonna happen.' But let's find out *what else is possible*. And let's give her a little love." The audience cheers her on and then I say, "Stop twisting. Open your eyes."

After thirty seconds of aimless moves, the volunteer has not made any progress toward matching colors on each side of the cube. Playfully I say, "Despite our positivity, no doubt that felt pointless—like you were spinning your wheels. Like it's even *further* away from being solved than before you started twisting. Like imperfection was inevitable." They usually laugh a little and nod their head. I then say to the volunteer, "You probably don't realize it, but you *did* solve the cube." You can probably imagine her look of confusion. "Many times, we have a preconceived notion about what success looks like, and it can be hard to break free from old paradigms. When I instructed you to solve the cube, you probably thought I meant to make each side all the same color, right?"

"Right."

"That was a fair assumption, but what if what I actually meant was to match one of the sides of your cube perfectly to one of the sides of my cube?" Now, remember that the second cube has been in plain sight the entire time and has clearly not been messed with. I pick it up from the table and hold it side by side with the volunteer's cube in front of the close-up camera for all to see. Both cubes are mixed, but they match perfectly. For example, both might have a yellow square in the top left corner, a red one in the middle, and a white one in the bottom right, and so on.

Gasps.

"Or two sides?" I then rotate both cubes to reveal that the second faces of each cube also match each other perfectly. Again, mixed, but matched. More gasps. "What if each and every move you made got you more and more aligned with a greater vision than you could have imagined possible? A new picture of how things might be. A change no one sees coming. An opportunity to create something colorful, fun, and unexpected, encouraging others to look at things in a new way."

As I say this, I show that the third, fourth, fifth, and sixth sides of the cubes all match perfectly as well.

"Let's give her a hand—she crushed it!" The volunteer receives a big round of applause as she takes her seat.

I then say to the audience, "Who defines your success? You do. Don't let other people define it for you."

"Here's something else you should know about Rubik's cubes: Accomplished solvers, aka speedcubers, solve the cube in an average of fifty-five to sixty moves. While that's impressive, the maximum number of turns it actually takes from any of the forty-three quintillion positions is mathematically proven to be twenty. That's known as God's number. And get this—most of the time, you're far fewer than twenty moves away from solving it. You're closer to a breakthrough than you think."

"Surprising, right? You know what's also surprising and encouraging? How close you are to many solutions in your life and work, even though you may seem far from them at times."

I then put one of the cubes down and hold the other up to the camera. This next part makes for a great summary of my keynote presentation as well as for this book.

I begin twisting the cube with just one hand as I say these final words:

"Even when things seem imperfect at best—and completely messed up at worst . . ."

"If you start ugly, start small, and pick up the ball . . ." Twist.

"If you Always Give Thanks . . ." Twist.

"If you Pause, Pivot, and Pull . . ." Twist.

"And share your magic with everyone around you . . ." Twist.

"Then you can single-handedly prove *what else is possible.*" Twist.

At that point, believe it or not, the Rubik's Cube has been solved in the traditional form, with solid-colored sides all around.

Something greater is always possible.

Some Possibilities Live Into Eternity: In Honor of Ivy

SOON AFTER I finished the major revisions for this book, my world came crashing down. We lost our eight-week-old baby, Ivy. Losing a child has always been my greatest fear. After years of speaking to audiences about resilience and accepting challenges head-on, I was unexpectedly presented with the biggest challenge of my life. As I write this, it has been three months and three weeks since Ivy passed, and the pain is still fresh.

I'm sharing this with you to show you how the possibility mindset goes far beyond overcoming failure or looking to your next level of greatness. I want you to know that asking *What else is possible?* is especially helpful when you're living through your worst nightmare and how it might even save your life and impact your eternal existence. I hope the story of what happened and what follows offers you hope in your hardest times.

Ivy Eloise Henderson is our 8th daughter, and she was born August 8th, 2024. Eight weeks later, I was driving home from a local performance in Kansas City when I got a phone call from my neighbor: "Hey, you on your way home?"

Something was wrong. I could hear it in his voice. Then he said it. "Lynn laid Ivy down for a nap, and when she checked on her . . . she wasn't breathing. They're placing her in the ambulance, and Lynn and Claire are riding in the police car to the hospital."

I said, "Shoot me straight Pete—how bad is it?"

"It's not good. They're breathing for her right now," he said.

The world stopped. My thoughts spiraled to the worst-case scenario: *She's not gonna make it. I can't deal with this. This can't be happening.* I sped to the hospital and got there just after Lynn and Claire. I had never seen such a hopeless and helpless expression as I saw on Lynn's face in that moment.

She said, "She might be gone." I thought, *Lord, please save her.*

They took us to a room with a chaplain. Our only question was: How is she? A staff member had left to check. When she came back, she said: "If you want to see her, now is the time."

As they escorted us to Ivy's room, our point person held Lynn's hand, and said, "I need you to breathe." The room was filled with nurses and hospital staff, all working hard—but nobody made eye contact with us.

We moved past all the people, and then there she was. My baby. Lying there. Unresponsive. A tube down her throat. An IV in Ivy's little arm. A tiny diaper, her clothes cut off in the chaos to save her. Sweet little onesie. Precious little pants now torn and bloodstained from the needle jab.

No, no. Come on, Ivy. God, bring her back. We can't lose her. Compressions. Breaths. Heart monitor. No activity. It was surreal. *This can't be happening. Not to us. Not to her. Stay calm. Devin, be strong. Come on, Ivy.*

"Can we talk to her?"

"Yes, absolutely."

"Ivy. Hey Ivy, it's us. We love you. Come back to us. Can you hear us? It's Mom and Dad. We love you so much. Just breathe for us, honey."

Nothing. More compressions, breaths, defibrillator. *Come on heart monitor—give us a sign, anything.*

And then our point person calmly said: "We've been working for an hour and we haven't gotten a heartbeat. I'm so sorry. We're going to have to call it." That was at 9:01 p.m. on October 3rd, 2024.

I'm the kind of person who trusts that everything happens for a reason. There are no coincidences. But when something like this happens, the questions come: Why? What's the purpose in this pain? How do I go on living? I've asked them all. And then in the middle of my deepest grief, another question emerged:

What else is possible?

What if there *was* some reason this was meant to be? What if there *was* a purpose in our pain? What if this moment, as devastating as it was, could somehow make life richer than ever before?

I never could've asked those questions without the possibility mindset, because embedded within it is something deeper: faith. Now, I realize your spiritual views may be different from mine. I respect that, so I won't get super specific about my faith, but I will share what gave me strength to break through my hardest moments.

I believe the fingerprints of something greater are all over this world. Many times, they're invisible, but if you dust for the fingerprints, they become apparent. And when I started dusting, I saw something incredible. I saw the number 8. I saw the number 8 over and over. And all of a sudden, 8 was more than a number, it was a signature:

Ivy wasn't just the 8th of 8 children, she was the 8th of 8 girls. She was born on August 8th—the 8th day of the 8th month. She lived on this earth 8 weeks to the day.

Ivy was providentially laid to rest in section 8 of a memory garden at the feet of her Grandpa Bill, who passed away in 2018 at the age of 88. His father, Ivy's great-grandpa Cole, also died at the age of 88.

We recently learned that the children's wing of our church was dedicated on Ivy's birthday, August 8th, or again, 8/8, twenty years before she was born.

Our friends gave us memorial bracelets with ivy leaves, and there just happens to be 8 leaves on the bracelets. That wasn't planned—at least not by our friends.

And as it turns out, the number 8 reveals that I've been gearing up for this moment my whole life.

I've played piano since kindergarten, and you may know a piano has 88 keys.

My jersey number for soccer in high school was 8.

My first car was an 88 Accord.

Back to the Future was my favorite movie growing up, and the speed that makes time travel possible is 88 mph.

Once I started sharing this story in my keynote presentations, the 8s just kept coming. After one presentation, a woman named Charisse thanked me. She said it meant a lot. She was also one of 8 siblings, and as a child, her family experienced a loss too—her younger brother, Brent, died in a bicycle accident. He was 8.

Another time, Matt approached me and said the whole "8 thing" blew his mind—and felt deeply personal. His brother, Ivan—a name remarkably close to Ivy's—was also born on August 8th and graduated high school in 1988.

Not long after that, Elizabeth shared with me that her precious baby, Dante, was one of eight siblings. He lived for eight months and eight days—and was the eighth person in the world to pass away from his condition. On top of that, his brother had always worn the number eight on his football jersey—even before Dante's passing.

And just recently, a woman named Randy sent me this message:

> "When you mentioned Ivy, time stood still. I'm sure many hearts stopped for a moment. Tears were shed. It became clear that anyone can overcome the worst life has to offer. But your story hit extra close to home for me because, you see, I have a grandbaby named Ivy. She's 8 months old."

Some say the number 8 symbolizes new beginnings. We believe Ivy's life is already blessing so many people with a beautiful beginning of their own—and in that way, she's leaving an eternal legacy. And of course, when you turn the number 8 on its side, it becomes the infinity symbol—a powerful reminder of the unlimited possibilities her life continues to inspire.

If you've experienced a significant loss or any other extremely difficult situation, I encourage you to start dusting for fingerprints. It may not appear in the form of a number like it did for me, and it may not be as obvious—I don't know why I was blessed with the number 8. Maybe it was simply what I needed. But I believe that if you start dusting, something will eventually come into view. Something meant just for you.

And as you search for meaning, remember this: Faith transforms your perspective. Faith is the reality of what we hope for, it's the proof of what we *don't* see. Because of faith, our family doesn't grieve like people who have no hope. We have the peace that passes understanding. We believe Ivy is in a better place, and that gives us great joy—even in our grief. Yes, the pain is real. But we'll see her again soon. Life is short—like a mist that appears for a little while and then it's gone.

And if this life is short, then what am I going to do with the time I have left? Surviving would be an ordinary goal. But what would be a seemingly impossible goal?

How about experiencing a more abundant life than ever before and helping others do the same? How about building a marriage that's stronger than I could ever imagine? What about cherishing every moment with the people we love? We value our children greatly, whether they're here with us in this life or waiting for us in the next. What if my life—and my purpose—were forever changed for the better because of Ivy? What if, even in the face of great loss, something beautiful could be born from the pain?

That's what I choose to believe. That's how I choose to live. And I hope and pray you'll do the same.

What else is possible?

Acknowledgments

To model after the *Wizard of Oz* cast appreciating the stagehands, I want to *point* to the ones who made this book possible by caringly and lovingly pulling my ropes behind the scenes.

I owe my "magical journey" to so many remarkable people. As I wrote about those early years of inspiration, I was overwhelmed with gratitude for the right people showing up at the right time—people who encouraged me, deepened my passion for the art of magic, and kept me moving forward as that passion gradually became both a career and a lifelong calling. From childhood supporters to world-class mentors, each one played a vital role. I'm also deeply grateful to legendary magicians like Jeff McBride, Lance Burton, and André Kole—true giants whose influence shaped not just my technique, but my belief in what was possible. While they weren't mentioned earlier, their example shaped my journey in ways just as profound. I also owe thanks to the many patient friends and strangers who graciously allowed me to "borrow" their watches without holding it against me.

A big point to the many clients, conference coordinators, and speaker bureau representatives who have welcomed me to their stages and believed in my message. Their confidence has played an immeasurable role in making this book possible. The stories and skills I've honed over two decades are now shared in these pages, allowing me to inspire even those I may never meet in person.

And I'll never forget early believers like J. W. White, Cathy Edwards, and Roman Madrigal—some of my very first clients—who took a chance on me when all I had was a dream and a deck of cards. They laid the foundation for everything that followed. Each person, each interaction, was a gift—another step on the bridge between imagination and reality. Without them, and others like them, this journey wouldn't just look different—it might not have existed at all.

A heartfelt appreciation goes out to my speaking coach and friend, Danielle Ross, whose wisdom and encouragement have been a guiding force through many professional and personal decisions. She not only helped shape my keynote into the impactful presentation it is today but inadvertently left her touch on these very pages. I also want to recognize her husband, Chris, whose steadfast support has not gone unnoticed.

I'm deeply grateful to Streamline Books and their incredible team for equipping me with the tools and support needed to accomplish what at times felt like a seemingly impossible goal. To cofounders Will Severns and Alex Demczak—thank you for creating such a smooth and empowering pathway for getting a book to print. Justin Pickens, I'm grateful for the spark you provided that helped launch this journey. A big thanks to Donnel McLohon for your devotion and steady support from beginning to end. And to my patient, grace-giving editor-in-chief, Traci Matt—thank you for transforming what could have been a grueling process into an unexpectedly joyful journey.

As I was finalizing this book, our family faced the greatest trial of our lives. Ivy's blessed coming and going brought everything to a halt. But through the love and support of so many, I was able to pick up the ball—or pen—and follow it to completion. I am forever grateful to Crystal Day, my booking coordinator, who stepped up for me in the middle of that storm with generosity and unwavering support. To all who uplifted us—through love offerings, meals, prayers, and countless acts of kindness—you have blessed us beyond words. And to our dear friends and family who grieved with us, surrounded us with love, and filled our hearts with encouragement and words of truth—you helped us walk through the valley rather than lie down and sink into it.

A massive debt of gratitude goes to my parents, Bill and Ginger Henderson. I couldn't have done this without you—any of it. The soccer, the magic, the speaking, the career, my faith—you shaped, believed in, and supported me every step of the way. Dad, I miss you dearly and can't wait to see you again. To my awesome siblings Jason and Gretchen, I cherish the memories we made when we were young and still cherish you today. Thank you for watching "that neat magic trick" over and over again through the years. Your influence and love have helped weave the fabric of my being and I'm forever grateful to have you both in my life. And Mom, simply put, you are *the best* mother a boy and man could ever have. There's just no better way to say it—you are the wind beneath my wings.

To our precious baby girls—I say your names in age order so regularly in my prayers they roll off my tongue like water over smooth stones: Claire, Charlotte, Cambry, Elsie, Eva, Emme, Haven, and Ivy. This paragraph could be a book all its own—no, a book series—that would make the *Magic Tree House* series look like a single note in a symphony. It would be a series devoted entirely to how deeply I love, treasure, and adore you. I write this through tears, overwhelmed with gratitude for every one of you, and I can't—and don't want to—imagine this life without you. Thank you for graciously allowing me to share our experiences together in my keynote and in this book. Your brilliant and precious thinking make for incredible and entertaining life lessons, to say the least. Each of your beautiful spirits and one-of-a-kind personalities has taught me, shaped me, and made me a better person.

The tears of gratitude stream on as I try to decide where to start with thanking the incredible mother of my children, my beautiful wife and best friend. Lynn, if I had a penny for every time you graciously allowed me to bounce an idea off you for a business decision, a branding or marketing move, keynote content, which stories to include in this book, if a joke was funny enough, if a magic trick was tricky enough, which clothes I should wear on stage or how I should cut my hair, I could retire now from speaking and buy us an island. You've never minded frustrating me with honest answers, which is *exactly* what I've always needed to achieve the next level of greatness. Sharing life with you has been an indescribable joy, and having you alongside me in business has kept me going during the times I've questioned everything I'm doing. You have given me an unusual amount of grace, been a rock for me in so many ways, and kept me grounded in truth over the years. Our date nights, getaways, cribbage games, morning walks, and your smile are each worth living for. I love you—always have, always will.

And last but certainly not least, my deepest gratitude goes to the Master Author, who continues to write new chapters in my life—each one rich with hope, purpose, and profound lessons to share. As the plot deepens and unfolds, may His hand continue to guide me as I tell my story in a way that helps others believe something greater is always possible.

About the Author

Devin Henderson is a powerhouse of talent, a sought-after keynote speaker, and a master of inspiring greatness. With over two decades of experience, he has captivated thousands as an award-winning comedian, magician, and motivational speaker, earning the prestigious CSP (Certified Speaking Professional) designation from the National Speakers Association—one of the highest honors in the industry.

Devin's passion is helping individuals and organizations unlock their greatest potential and develop the resilience to push forward, no matter the challenge. Through a one-of-a-kind experience blending heartfelt storytelling, humor, audience interaction, and mind-blowing magic, he empowers audiences to defy limits in business and life. His presentations have been described as "unreal," "unexpected," and "unforgettable."

A trusted speaker for Fortune 500 companies and leading organizations and associations, Devin delivers transformative insights that leave a lasting impact. He and his incredible wife are proud parents of eight beautiful children—seven on earth and one in heaven. They live in Shawnee, Kansas, where family remains at the heart of everything they do.

Book Devin for your conference at DevinHenderson.com.

www.ingramcontent.com/pod-product-compliance
Lightning Source LLC
Chambersburg PA
CBHW020352130626
46549CB00006B/2271